# Going to the Sources

---

Arthur S. Link,
GENERAL EDITOR FOR HISTORY

# Going to the Sources

## A Guide to Historical Research and Writing

Anthony Brundage
California State Polytechnic University, Pomona

Harlan Davidson, Inc.
Arlington Heights, Illinois 60004

**Library of Congress Cataloging in Publication Data**

Brundage, Anthony, 1938–
    Going to the sources : a guide to historical research and writing
    Anthony Brundage.
        p.   cm.
    ISBN 0-88295-865-8 (pbk.) :
    1. History—Methodology.   2. History—Research.
3. Historiography.   I. Title.
D16.B893  1989          907'.2—dc19          88-30883
                                                    CIP

Cover design: Roger Eggers

Manufactured in the United States of America
97 96 95 94 93    MG    4 5 6 7 8

To My Students

# Contents

# Preface

THIS BOOK was developed out of a course on "History Methods" that I have taught to upper-division history majors during the past dozen years. As anyone who has taught a methodology course can attest, it can be either a uniquely rewarding or deeply frustrating experience; usually it is both. Typically, students approach the course with some apprehension. Up to this point, their academic encounters with history have been chiefly in the form of lecture-discussion courses, a format with which they feel relatively secure. In the "History Methods" class they find themselves on unfamiliar terrain, confronted with new and sometimes perplexing challenges. Fortunately, often mingled with this feeling of apprehension is a sense of excitement about the prospect of achieving new levels of understanding of their chosen discipline as well as acquiring a new set of research and writing skills. It was in the hope of fostering the excitement, allaying the apprehension, and developing the skills that I undertook the writing of this book.

Central to my own sense of the excitement of history is an appreciation of it as open-ended and dynamic. Developing that awareness in others is an important source of satisfaction for me as a teacher of history. I have therefore structured this book around the concept of history as a dynamic process. The common tendency to view history as fixed and static is best overcome by exploring the ways in which historians actually go about examining the past, constantly searching for fresh patterns and meanings and developing new methodologies to achieve them. Accordingly, an introductory chapter on historiography (the history of history writing) sets the stage for a discussion of the types of historical sources and the organization of the historical profession in the next chapter. I have found that a discussion of the structure of the profession itself is an effective method of explaining the nature, significance, and uses of the various kinds of sources.

Chapter 3, on how to locate sources, is the central chapter as far as research methods are concerned. It is a detailed, practical guide through the various resources that enable students to identify and obtain the essential books, articles, essays, and other materials relating to their topic. I have tried to avoid overloading it with too many details, recognizing that it could easily turn into a dense technical treatise. My purpose is to provide the reader with a basic blueprint of the information retrieval systems available to historians. Once students have acquired this knowledge, they can locate the essential bibliography on any historical topic, without having to be directed to the major scholarly works by a specialist in the field. Indeed, helping the reader to acquire the ability to operate as a competent, self-directed researcher is one of the principal goals of this book.

Another major goal is to introduce students to some of the fundamentals of writing history. Chapters 4 and 5 explore the methods of writing two common types of paper, the historiographic essay and the research paper. This follows the sequence of my own teaching, in which a historiographic essay (based chiefly on secondary sources) is the centerpiece of the "History Methods" class, while a longer research paper (using primary as well as secondary sources) is assigned in the senior thesis and seminar. Useful as I find this sequence, there is nothing sacrosanct about it. Each instructor will have his or her own preference as to the type of paper assigned and could, for example, move without difficulty directly from Chapter 3 to Chapter 5. That portion of Chapter 4 explaining how to find secondary sources for a particular topic could be used, but the following section on the details of writing a historiographic essay could be omitted. Chapter 6 recapitulates some of the major points made in the book, in particular the theme of the open-ended nature of history. The achievement of creative insights and analyses is shown to be closely linked to the concept of history as a dynamic intellectual discipline.

Both of the major components of the historian's craft—research and writing—are difficult and demanding. They are also immensely rewarding. I hope that this book proves to be an efficient, stimulating guide to a discipline that is still one of our surest and most satisfying methods of understanding human affairs.

# 1

# The Ever-Changing Shape
# and Texture of the Past

## Static and Dynamic Concepts of History

A RECENT cocktail party conversation made me acutely aware of some
common misconceptions of my chosen field of study. After being introduced to a psychologist, I listened with keen interest to his enthusiastic account of some of the latest approaches and interpretations in
his discipline. Having expostulated on this topic with obvious relish,
he said: "I don't suppose there's much new going on in your field."
Stunned by this remark, I scrutinized his face carefully for signs of
either humor or intended offense. Seeing neither, I was forced to conclude that he genuinely believed history to be a passive if not dormant
discipline. I attempted to disabuse him of this unfortunate view by
explaining some of the exciting developments in a few of the most
active new areas of historical study—social history, women's history,
cliometrics, and psychohistory. Our discussion of the last of these categories produced a detectable flash of interest, and I would like to think
that he has now begun to question whether history is quite the fixed,
dull chronicle he had imagined it to be.

Reflecting later on this encounter, I realized that my companion's
attitude was by no means unusual, even among educated persons. The
reasons for this are not far to seek. The popular conception of history
as simply a record of past events seems to have as an obvious corollary
its basic unchangeability. History is seen as a vast array of facts, arranged
more or less chronologically, unalterable except by the occasional
unearthing of a lost city or discovery of a trunkful of letters in an attic.
At its best, it is an exciting and vivid costume drama; at its worst, a
tedious, turgid catalog of dates and names designed to torment the
young. One should not be surprised that it is the latter viewpoint that

predominates. Not only is modern American culture remorselessly present-minded, but the teaching and examining of history in our schools often reinforces this attitude.

Things tend to improve at the college level, and those who have not already developed an attitude of unremitting hostility to history often discover an exciting new set of intellectual challenges and vistas. Yet even at this level, introductory courses sometimes only confirm students' negative attitudes. It is not a question of bad teaching; knowledgeable, enthusiastic, and articulate history teachers abound at all levels. The problem lies in presenting history as a story with a fixed plot and cast of characters. It is true that this approach is natural and to some extent unavoidable, particularly for students receiving their first systematic exposure to history. But it is also possible, indeed critically important, to offer at least a glimpse of a very different concept—history as a dynamic process. This means a rich, varied, evolving intellectual process with which one achieves a deeper and better understanding of the world. It is historical in that it deals with the past, but it conceptualizes the past as being in a constant dialog with an ever-advancing present, responding to new questions and revealing fresh patterns to illuminate the human condition. This is history as understood by professional historians, and it is high time that others were let in on the secret.

This concept of history stands in sharp contrast to the static one that prevails when history is thought of merely as a fixed story. The past becomes kaleidoscopic, offering different patterns and answers to each inquirer. This should not be taken to mean that each person can fashion whatever he or she wishes and call it history. There are rigorous procedures to be observed in the framing of historical questions, in the selection and interpretation of sources, and in the presentation of one's findings. Not everyone finds the dynamic concept of history appealing. There is, after all, something comforting about the supposed unchangeability of the past. To shift from the static to the dynamic mode can be as disconcerting as awakening to the fact that the terra firma on which we walk masks an array of seething, grinding tectonic plates (an example that occurs readily to a native Californian). The difference of course is that while shifting tectonic plates seem to promise only devastating earthquakes, the concept of a changing past offers immense intellectual rewards.

## Revisionism

A concept central to an appreciation of history as process is revisionism. This means an unending search by historians for fresh sources, approaches, methodological concepts, and interpretations. On the basis of these changing materials and methods, historians are able to offer an ever-new past to the present. Or rather, they offer a multitude of new pasts, since each historian's view of the past is at least slightly different from another's, sometimes dramatically different. In other words, a vigorous, many-sided debate among scholars is not only inescapable but essential.

Revisionism has been practiced since at least the time of the Greeks, as anyone who has examined the history of history-writing is aware, but it has become particularly pronounced in the last few centuries, with the dramatic transformations in social, economic, and political life. As the pace of change quickens and its magnitude increases, there is a corresponding pressure to revise our accounts of the past. This is because one of the most fundamental dimensions of our identity is provided by history, and as we change, it too must be transformed. When America was a simple agrarian society, without large cities, complex technology, and a vital world role, one kind of history sufficed. As the country grew, industrialized, and developed an array of perplexing social problems, new questions about the past had to be asked: What distinctive features were to be found on the frontier, and how had these affected national life and character? What was the historical experience of hitherto disempowered or exploited groups—blacks, native Americans, or women? What were the historic patterns of relationship between social classes, and how were they changing? How was America's posture vis-à-vis the rest of the world being altered? These are only a few of the questions that began to be asked during the last century. Not surprisingly, a multiplicity of new approaches and interpretations were offered, and hitherto neglected records and remnants of the past became primary source material.

America did not initiate these new ways of looking at the past. Many European societies had begun to experience social and economic change earlier, and this was reflected in their historical accounts. The philosophes of the European Enlightenment developed a decidedly revisionist view of history and used it to great effect in their campaign against ignorance, superstition, and tyranny. Writers such as Voltaire

and Gibbon broke with long-established tendencies to write reveren-
tially about states, rulers, and legal and ecclesiastical institutions. Their
works, still rightly regarded as great classics in the writing of history,
served as manifestoes in the eighteenth-century struggle to advance the
cause of liberty and reason.

## Malthus, Marx, and New Forms of Historical Consciousness

With the advent of the Industrial Revolution and attendant political
unrest and demographic change at the end of the eighteenth century,
some writers were moved to ask novel questions about the past. Thomas
Malthus, that "gloomy" economist who began to point with alarm to
the rapid and accelerating growth of population, complained that "the
histories of mankind which we possess are, in general, histories only
of the higher classes." He went on to suggest a history of the habits
and mores of the general population based on accurate statistical information. Malthus was well aware of the massive intellectual labors
that would have to be expended on this project, but called upon future
scholars to shoulder the burden:

> A satisfactory history of this kind, of one people and of one period, would
> require the constant and minute attention of many observing minds in
> local and general remarks on the state of the lower classes of society, and
> the causes that influenced it; and to draw accurate inferences upon this
> subject, a succession of such historians for some centuries would be nec-
> essary.[1]

Thus almost two hundred years ago, Malthus outlined an agenda for
the diligent historical demographers and social historians of our time
whose labors are bearing rich fruit. Fortunately, the invention of the
computer has significantly shortened the time he predicted would be
required for such investigations.

The miseries of the early Industrial Revolution, coupled with the rise
of a large, militant working class, led others to look for the historic
roots of social conflict. Karl Marx is beyond question the most important of these commentators, and historical studies have been im-

---

[1]Thomas Malthus, *An Essay on Population* (London: J. M. Dent, 1952; first published
1798), vol. I, 16.

mensely enriched by his powerful and trenchant analyses. When he and Friedrich Engels issued *The Communist Manifesto* in 1848, it was intended as a clarion call to arms, not a work of scholarship. But the *Manifesto's* claim that all of human history is a history of class struggle represents perhaps the most sweeping statement of historical revisionism ever offered. This served as the interpretive framework for all of their scholarly writings.

Marx's insistence that each historical epoch can be properly understood only by reference to its economic and material bases has profoundly altered the discipline of history. Virtually all subsequent historians, most of whom would object to being described as Marxists, are deeply in his debt. It is not a question of embracing Marxism as an ideology or of accepting its vision of the future, elements that can be readily detached from the Marxist perspective on the past. The point is that Marx, like Malthus, forced us to question whether humanity is really well served by confining its historical attention to the doings of kings, statesmen, and generals. It is by no means the case that political history, military history, or biography has withered on the vine as a result of these new perspectives. But some of the best work being done in these traditional forms of history is the better for taking economic and social forces into account. Overall, the juxtaposition of the old forms with the new perspectives has created a complex, many-faceted debate—another manifestation of the vitality of history as process.

## Toward a "People's History"

I do not mean to suggest that without Malthus or Marx, historians would have continued in their accustomed mold. Society was being transformed in too many ways for this to have been possible; the emergence of a variety of new approaches was inevitable. An example is provided by a maverick English clergyman named John Richard Green, who in 1874 published a very influential book entitled *A Short History of the English People*. Green declared in the preface to his work:

> I have preferred to pass lightly and briefly over the details of foreign wars and diplomacies, the personal adventures of kings and nobles, the pomp of courts, or the intrigues of favourites, and to dwell at length on the

incidents of that constitutional, intellectual, and social advance in which we read the history of the nation itself.[2]

The emphasis in the title was on the word "People," and the author clearly believed that he was shifting the spotlight away from the historic elites to the mass of the population.

While many consider Green's *Short History* to be less innovative than he claimed, the book was enormously successful because the late nineteenth century public thought he was breaking new ground in a way they considered necessary and important. It was reprinted sixteen times before the second edition appeared, posthumously, in 1887. Numerous pirated editions were published in the United States, and, before the end of the century, Italian, French, German, Russian, and Chinese translations appeared. Such an astonishing publishing success was due to something more than Green's literary gifts. Much of the world was then in the grip of vigorous populist and nationalist impulses, and the idea of a history of a people proved irresistibly attractive. It was a history, or rather a kind of history, whose time had come.

Needless to say, Green's *Short History* did not put an end to revisionism—no work ever has or will. It might even be said to have intensified the ferment and accelerated the revisionist process. By making the "People" the centerpiece of historical inquiry, a number of essential questions were begged. Just who were the "People"? Were they the entire population, or some segment of it—workers or the middle class, perhaps? Was the focus to be on city dwellers or peasants? Should ethnic or religious minorities be taken into account? What about women, never a minority but hitherto ignored by historians? Furthermore, Green's focus on the English people implied that nation-states were the appropriate units of historical investigation, yet there are many alternatives ranging from local communities to regions to the entire world.

## Minorities and Women Enter History

Revisionist efforts to recover and develop the history of minorities have necessarily often worked closely with political movements for the expansion of civil rights and the attainment of economic and social equal-

---

[2]John Richard Green, *A Short History of the English People* (New York: Harper and Brothers, 1899; first published 1874), xvii.

ity. Thus in the early decades of this century the great black American historian W. E. B. Du Bois was a major figure in the struggle for racial equality as well as an effective and dedicated scholar. His own writings, along with his participation in the founding of *The Journal of Negro History,* enhanced the visibility of blacks and rescued their history from the patronizing or frankly racist attitudes of most white historians of the period. An expansion of interest in black history during the last several decades obviously is linked to the intensification of the struggle for civic, social, and economic equality. In revealing the historic patterns of race relations, this new body of scholarship has served to enhance the pride and clarify the goals of black Americans. Moreover, it has educated white Americans about the nature and consequences of racism, thereby fostering progress toward a society of greater justice and opportunity. Much the same can be said of the burgeoning scholarship on the history of Hispanics, Native Americans, and other ethnic minorities.

Women's history has been particularly active during the last few decades and, like the history of ethnic minorities, can be correlated to vigorous political and social movements. Since historical invisibility is a virtually universal corollary to powerlessness, the campaign to establish gender equality necessarily required a historical component. Just as the "People" in the title of John Richard Green's history served as a rallying cry for populist and national groups earlier, June Sochen's *Herstory* (1974) did the same for the women's movement. Although there had been many important works in women's history before hers, the title of Sochen's book evoked in a single word the necessity for a story very different from that told by male historians.[3]

It should not be imagined that histories of minorities or women are designed as appendages to political causes. The same demanding criteria regarding the evaluation of sources, the marshalling of evidence, and the deployment of literary skill are used in assessing these histories as in any other. A blend of diligence, skepticism, imagination, judiciousness, and humor pays the same big dividends to historians in these fields as it does in others. Nor should these developing bodies of scholarship be seen as representing some new ethnic or gender-related orthodoxy. They are no more monolithic than any other field of history. Indeed,

---

[3]June Sochen, *Herstory: A Woman's View of American History* (New York: Alfred Publishing Co., 1974).

some of the most vigorous and fruitful debates within the profession occur in these areas.

One important point of disagreement involves the same concern manifested in the nineteenth century over whether to focus on an elite or the masses of the population. Many of the earlier studies tended to concentrate on the achievements of extraordinary individual women or members of ethnic minorities. But critics have recently charged that, whatever the merits of these works in producing role models, they often serve to obscure the historical realities of the lives of the masses of the disempowered. There is a detectable shift in recent women's and minority history toward incorporating some of the methods and approaches of social history. This particular application of "history from below" exemplifies not only revisionism but also the process of cross-fertilization among various fields of history.

So far the examples of historical scholarship that have been examined, while exhibiting the concept of history as a dynamic process, can be fitted into the "history as story" format in the broadest sense. That is, most of them have a narrative structure in which a sequence of connected events occurring within a span of time is deployed by the historian to create pattern and meaning. Even when large social aggregates such as classes or ethnic groups rather than individuals are the centerpiece, they can still usually be made to function as characters in a complex story. Marx's scheme of history is a good example, with (at one stage) its rising bourgeoisie deployed against a crumbling feudal nobility. The unfolding of his story of conflict is marked by such significant events or movements as the growth of towns, the Protestant Reformation, the invention of the steam engine, and the French Revolution. But the twentieth century has witnessed the creation of varieties of history that largely or completely abandon the investigation of change over time. We will briefly examine two of them—the *Annales* school and cliometrics.

## The *Annales* School and Cliometrics

A historical journal established in France in 1929 provided the forum for a new kind of historical scholarship, one that aimed at nothing less than recapturing the totality of human experience. By employing the methods and techniques of the social sciences, the scholars connected to this new enterprise sought to delineate all aspects of past societies, with an emphasis on those enduring patterns of culture that changed slowly if at all. The journal was called *Annales d'histoire économique et sociale*, hence practitioners of this kind of history came to be called Annalistes. Central to this approach was a disparagement of event-oriented history. Those innumerable events that historians had charged with significance and arranged in various configurations to produce history were regarded by the Annalistes as mere surface ripples. The traditional concern with events was replaced by a search for society's *mentalités*, the ways of life and values that persisted despite major upheavals.

One of the foremost Annalistes was Fernand Braudel, whose magisterial study, *The Mediterranean and the Mediterranean World in the Age of Philip II*, appeared in 1949. Braudel's revisionism involved not only the emphasis on persistent patterns of life but also the use of the Mediterranean basin as the setting for his analysis, rather than some political entity such as Spain or France. A favorite phrase of Braudel and other Annalistes was the *longue durée*, a vast sweep of time during which little change occurred. Regarding the difficulty in gaining acceptance for this perspective in the profession, Braudel commented:

> For the historian, accepting the longue durée entails a readiness to change his style, his attitudes, a whole reversal in his thinking, a whole new way of conceiving social affairs. It means becoming used to a slower tempo, which sometimes almost borders on the motionless.[4]

Although Braudel himself by no means neglected "events" altogether, it is clear that the Annaliste approach in its purest form tends virtually to preclude any sense of history as story.

A close partnership between historians and other social scientists is an important tenet of the Annales school. The attempt to delineate cultural patterns with little attention to change over time is an approach similar to that employed by many anthropologists and sociologists. An even newer field of history called cliometrics evinces a similar determination to utilize social science methodologies. Clio was the Greek muse of history; thus cliometricians are those scholars who employ quantification to reveal historical pattern and meaning. Obviously some-

---

[4]Fernand Braudel, *On History*, translated by Sarah Matthews (Chicago: University of Chicago Press, 1980), 33.

thing a good deal more is requisite than an ability or willingness to count, which historians have been doing since Herodotus. Cliometricians use computers, sophisticated programs, and social science models. They also tend to disparage source material that cannot be quantified, so that most of the records relied upon by other historians in fashioning their accounts are devalued as "soft" or "impressionistic" evidence, to be used reluctantly and in strict subordination to the numeric data. Clearly, only those areas of historical study for which there is an abundance of records yielding quantifiable data are amenable to such an approach. For this reason, economic history has been a particularly active area of investigation—and particularly controversial.

Among the most controversial of the cliometric studies is Robert Fogel's and Stanley Engerman's *Time on the Cross* (1974), a study of slavery in the United States. Deploying a formidable array of charts, graphs, and statistics, the authors set out to disprove a number of time-honored beliefs about slavery, such as its alleged inefficiency compared to a free economy. The picture of American slavery in *Time on the Cross* is that of a thriving, expanding institution in both its agricultural and industrial components. Besides promoting their own revisionist view of slavery, Fogel and Engerman made sweeping claims about the ability of cliometrics to transform economic history across a broad front:

> The cliometricians have downgraded the role of technological change in American economic advance; they have controverted the claim that railroads were necessary to the settlement and exploitation of the West; they have contended that the boom and bust of the 1830s and early 1840s were the consequences of developments in Mexico and Britain rather than the policies of Andrew Jackson; and they have rejected the contention that the Civil War greatly accelerated the industrialization of the nation.[5]

Despite such a ringing assertion, none of these new interpretations has gone unchallenged. Indeed, a major counterattack across a broad front is under way, not only against some of the cliometricians' interpretations but against much of their methodology as well. Perhaps the most vigorous assault has come from Jacques Barzun, whose *Clio and the Doctors* appeared in the same year as Fogel and Engerman's study. Barzun makes an eloquent plea for keeping history within the tradition

---

[5]Robert Fogel and Stanley L. Engerman, *Time on the Cross: The Economics of American Negro Slavery*, 2 vols (Boston and Toronto: Little, Brown, & Co., 1974), vol I, 7.

of humane letters, resisting the temptation to use the latest piece of technology or scientific model. And, as the subtitle of his book indicates, Barzun had in mind not only the cliometricians but the psychohistorians as well.[6]

## Psychology and History

Psychohistory represents an attempt to apply to historical study the methods and insights developed by Freud and other psychological theorists during the past hundred years. In dealing with the question of motives, historians often have to look beneath the surface in an effort to discern the real as distinct from the alleged reason for an action or policy. Generally they recognize that to move beyond the manifest content of the sources tends to render such judgments tentative and problematic. Psychohistorians are less disposed to be tentative. Bolstered by a belief in the scientific soundness of clinical evidence, psychohistory undertakes to expose what is claimed to be the real but hitherto hidden face of the past. One of the most skilful and sensitive practitioners of psychobiography, the late Fawn Brodie, described in her revisionist study of Thomas Jefferson the nature of this approach as well as the barriers to its acceptance:

> The idea that a man's inner life affects every aspect of his intellectual life and also his decision-making should need no defense today. To illuminate this relationship, however, requires certain biographical techniques that make some historians uncomfortable. One must look for feeling as well as fact, for nuance and metaphor as well as idea and action.[7]

One important distinction between this field and some of the other newer forms that draw upon social science methodologies is that psychohistory is altogether compatible with history as story. Indeed, it has assisted in the revival of biography, a traditional genre much maligned by the Annalists and others. In some respects, psychobiography and the Annales school are poles apart—it is hard to imagine points of focus much different than the life of an individual on the one hand and the *mentalité* of a whole civilization during a vast sweep of time on the

---

[6]Jacques Barzun, *Clio and the Doctors: Psycho-History, Quanto-History, and History* (Chicago: University of Chicago Press, 1974).

[7]Fawn Brodie, *Thomas Jefferson: An Intimate History* (New York: Norton, 1974), 16.

other. Of course, psychohistorians are not necessarily biographers. The methods and insights of social psychology can provide an additional dimension to the study of social history—the phenomenon of crowd psychology during political upheavals, for example. They can prove useful to Annalistes as well, provided that the mass psychological patterns being examined are of an enduring nature.

## A Multitude of Avenues to the Past

It should not be imagined that this cursory survey of a few movements and trends can possibly delineate the enormous variety of approaches to and interpretations of the past. The foregoing examples of revisionism in the writing of history during the last couple of centuries were introduced in an attempt to illustrate the concept of history as a dynamic process. Clearly, "history as story" is not a declining or old-fashioned form. In spite of the appearance of new kinds of analysis, it seems likely that the narrative mode will remain dominant. What is crucial to grasp is that there is an enormous variety of narrative approaches and that new ones will continue to appear. There is, quite simply, no such thing as a "definitive" history of any topic. Although this term is sometimes applied to a particularly impressive work of scholarship, it would, if taken literally, foreclose all subsequent inquiry. History would then tend to become that static body of knowledge often imagined by those with too little exposure to it as a discipline.

Historiography, which in its broadest sense means the history of history writing, is a demanding and vitally important branch of the discipline of history. Students who have not taken a course in historiography before embarking upon advanced undergraduate research projects would be well-advised to read some of the general works on the subject.[8] It is important to have some notion of historiography in this broad sense before turning to bibliographic research on a given topic. When engaged in such a project, the term historiography will be encountered in its narrower meaning—the various ways scholars have

---

[8]See, for example, Ernst Breisach, *Historiography, Ancient, Medieval, and Modern* (Chicago: University of Chicago Press, 1983). A recent brief survey is Mark T. Gilderhus, *History and Historians: A Historiographical Introduction* (Englewood Cliffs, New Jersey: Prentice-Hall, 1987).

investigated and interpreted the topic. Each topic has its own historiography. An understanding of its dimensions is essential, not only for constructing a historiographic essay, but also for writing a research paper using primary sources. These are the two types of historical writing that will be explored in later chapters. Before undertaking the writing of either a historiographic essay or a research paper, it is necessary to know the types of historical sources and how to find them. The next two chapters will explore these topics.

# 2

## The Nature and Variety
## of Historical Sources

AS WAS seen in the first chapter, history is an intellectual discipline in which the process of revisionism is central. Historians are constantly reviewing and rethinking the past, discovering new patterns and meanings. In this process, they depend upon the tangible remains of the past for source materials. Any remnant of the past can serve the purpose. Although written records tend to predominate as source materials in most fields of history, in others (particularly ancient and medieval) there is often a heavy reliance on artifacts. Such materials are of importance to those studying modern history as well. Weapons, coins, household utensils, cathedrals, statues, and motion pictures can cast as much light on the past as diaries, letters, and newspapers. Whether these historical raw materials are written records or artifacts we refer to them as primary sources. The written histories that historians fashion from these materials in turn become sources for subsequent investigators. They are referred to as secondary sources.

### Primary Sources

Written primary sources can be divided into two major categories: manuscripts and published materials. For historians, a manuscript is any handwritten or typewritten record or communication that has not been printed or otherwise duplicated in significant quantities for public dissemination. It can be anything from a laundry list to the minutes of a cabinet meeting in the Oval Office. Usually manuscript materials were intended for private or at least restricted use, although something such as the notes for a speech that was never delivered would be included. A manuscript can be as intensely personal as a diary, or as institutional as a list of Egyptian temple scribes. There is virtually no kind of written record that has not been used, or might some day be used, as a primary source. As social history and other new approaches to the past evolve, even the seemingly most trivial or mundane remnants may acquire significance.

## Manuscript Sources

Most of our attention will be devoted to published primary sources, since researchers in university libraries usually have only limited access to manuscript materials. But in many cases, there may be significant manuscript collections close at hand. Perhaps your university library has a Special Collections or Manuscript department containing important materials. Some universities have Oral History collections—transcripts of recorded interviews, discussions, and reflections by men and women in many walks of life. Beyond the campus, there may be nearby community libraries, local historical societies, or private individuals with manuscript resources. Any of these might prove extremely rewarding, depending on your subject. A topic of local history is most likely to afford you the opportunity of getting your hands on manuscript materials. It is worthwhile investigating the availability of manuscript collections in your locality. It may even help determine your choice of topics, though it should be realized that access to many major manuscript collections is limited to professional historians and advanced graduate students.

## Published Sources

Turning our attention to the published primary sources, these can be divided into two categories: (1) manuscript materials such as letters, diaries, and memoranda, usually intended as private, sometimes intimate documents, often published after the death of their authors; (2) materials that were intended from the outset to be printed and made public—for example, newspapers, congressional debates, autobiographies, annual company reports, and the United States Census.

There are few major political figures in the modern world, particularly the United States, whose writings have not been published. Library shelves groan with the massive collected works of our major presidents and statesmen. Other important figures of world history are also well represented, so that those researching the activities of the wielders of power or shapers of opinion will usually find no shortage of published primary sources. While many of these writings were not, strictly speaking, intended for public consumption, it is scarcely surprising that they eventually appear in published form. Those attaining high office in the last century or so could hardly expect that their papers would remain confidential for very long after their deaths. Indeed, the measure of immortality attainable through the posthumous publication of one's collected papers is apt to be a component of political ambition. Some leaders might be considered as "playing to posterity"—at least part of the time. Their papers must therefore be read and judged with an additional measure of critical acumen.

The injunction to be critical of the papers of society's leaders applies with special force to memoirs and autobiographies published at the end of their careers. These require interpretive care on two grounds. First, they depend to a considerable extent on the author's ability to recall events much earlier in his or her life. There must always be a presumed erosion of reliability in such recollections, one that increases with time. Second, autobiographies and memoirs are usually self-serving, or at least should be assumed to be so. In publishing these accounts, politicians and other public leaders are anxious to secure their place in history. Certain episodes in their lives will therefore be given prominence and a highly favorable interpretation, while others will be slighted, distorted, or ignored altogether. The same applies to the various persons discussed in these accounts. However, this by no means renders memoirs or autobiographies worthless as source materials. Among other things, they provide invaluable insights into the personalities of leading figures. As with all source materials, however, the historian must begin by asking the purpose for which they were written or published and then proceed with an appropriate measure of caution and skepticism.

A skeptical approach is also in order for materials such as the published letters and diaries of public figures. These sources are perhaps more trustworthy in one respect, since they are contemporary with the events and not therefore subject to the corrosive effects of time on memory. But even in this case, one must consider the author's ignorance, self-deception, or casting of an anxious eye on posterity. Moreover, published source materials are frequently only a selection, and sometimes quite a small selection, of the total body of the subject's writings. One must therefore take into account the built-in bias of the selecting or editing process. How representative of the whole are the documents that are published? Did a favorably disposed editor (perhaps a member of the family) suppress unflattering material? Even the most professional and evenhanded editor must make painful choices about the materials to be left out. This is why historians always consult the largest and best-edited collection of primary sources available (assuming of course that they do not have access to the manuscripts).

Somewhat different considerations apply to those written primary sources particularly valued by social historians. The development of interest in "history from below" has encouraged the finding and publication of the writings of ordinary people who, presumably, never dreamed their words would be published. The chance survival and later publication of the diary of an American pioneer woman or the letters of a soldier in the Crimean War can vividly illuminate the lives and experiences of the anonymous masses. This does not mean, of course, that such writings can be accepted uncritically. While the authors of such documents were probably unconcerned about the opinion of posterity, they can be expected to exhibit the normal human biases and blind spots. These "shortcomings" need not necessarily get in the way of our understanding; they may indeed be precisely the sort of thing for which we are looking.

Let us now turn to primary sources materials such as newspapers, magazines, and official reports of governments and other institutions. Not only were these intended from the outset to be made public; in many cases they were designed to influence public opinion. This is certainly the case with newspapers, whose editorial policies must usually be taken into account by historians. Thus to accept a newspaper version of one of the Lincoln-Douglas debates without considering the paper's political orientation would be a major critical lapse. Even if there were no detectable bias, one would have to consider the problems inherent in relying upon a single reporter's account—for example, his vantage point, his ability to hear all that was said from the podium, the reactions of those in the crowd that were closest to him. Diligent historians assemble as many such accounts as they can, treating each of them critically, sorting out obvious biases and errors, and fashioning as accurate a reconstruction as possible.

Other examples of print media must be approached in much the same way. Magazines, journals, and pamphlets all offer a vast storehouse of facts and prejudices. Like newspapers, they can reveal a great deal that the authors and editors never intended. Popular literature, sheet music, sermons, and plays can tell us much about society's common, unexamined assumptions. Consider, for example, the value of sources like this for investigating nineteenth-century American attitudes regarding gender roles or racial stereotyping. It is necessary to read such material in two quite different ways. On the one hand, the historian must try to see it as contemporaries did, an approach that requires both knowledge and sympathy. Simultaneously, the material must be viewed through the critical, dispassionate eyes of a late twentieth-century analyst who is posing questions that nineteenth-century people could not or did not ask.

There is an enormous variety and range of primary sources, only a few of which have been discussed here. When undertaking a research paper on a particular topic, it is well to ponder the types of sources that might be used. A little investigation and imagination may make it possible to use new kinds of sources from those employed by previous scholars working on the same topic. Or it may enable you to approach the sources from a different perspective. Conversely, if you are trying to decide on what to write, an awareness of the enormous range of sources can point you toward highly interesting topics you might otherwise never consider.

## Secondary Works

Secondary works or sources come in a great variety—from multivolume works of collective scholarship to short essays, and from general histories to the most specialized monographs. Some of this variety will be considered by examining the different forms of written histories—books, essays, and articles.

## Books

Books are such a universal and commonplace feature of academic life that students seldom ponder their diversity or structure. One can begin consideration of the diversity of types of history books with the breadth or narrowness of the subject. The extremes would be a textbook on the history of the world from the advent of human life and a study of a single individual or small community over a short span of time. In between these extremes are histories of such entities as civilizations, regions, nation-states, or social classes. Moreover, the approach can be political, social, economic, cultural, or some combination of these. It can be narrative or analytical. The focus can be on individuals or social aggregates. The tone and style may be "popular" or "scholarly"—that is, it may be calculated to appeal to a wide, nonprofessional readership or it may bristle with footnotes, statistics, and closely reasoned analysis designed for the author's scholarly peers.

Another method of distinguishing between history books is whether they are based chiefly on primary sources or other secondary works. As a rule, the broader the topic, the more the author relies on secondary works. Thus a book with the title *A History of the World* (or even *A History of the United States*) will probably not have many primary sources in its bibliography. You can see this for yourself by examining the bibliographies of one of the textbooks you used in a history survey course. Notice that the author's (many textbooks have multiple authors) account is fashioned out of the more specialized studies of other historians. New editions of texts are issued not just to bring the story up to the present, but to revise in light of the recent specialized scholarship. In this way the fruits of the latest scholarship enter the general survey texts and hence the classroom.

Textbooks and other general accounts are sometimes referred to as works of synthesis, because they synthesize or bring together the more specialized works of others. The latter, especially when they are fairly narrow in scope and based on primary sources, are called monographs. Some monographs are simply detailed, narrative accounts of particular subjects, but others attempt to break fresh interpretive ground and are thus important vehicles for historical revisionism. This does not mean that works of synthesis do not offer revisionist interpretations. Many of the most important revisionist works are fresh ways of accommodating, analyzing, and integrating the recent monograph literature rather than new ways of interpreting primary sources. This discussion of monographs and works of synthesis implies a sharper barrier between them than in fact exists. Many histories cannot be so tidily classified. Furthermore, the author of even the narrowest monograph is expected to take fully into account the other specialized scholarship on the topic, that is, to place his or her analysis within a historiographic frame of reference.

The historian's craft, like any other academic field, is both an individual and a collective enterprise. The latter refers not only to the fact

that historians need and depend upon the contributions of other scholars. It refers also to the fact that many works of history are jointly
written. In some cases two or more scholars may work closely together
in both the research and writing. More commonly a general editor will
coordinate the efforts of a team of historians, each of whom is given
primary responsibility for a portion of the whole. A couple of examples
are *The Oxford History of England* and *The Cambridge History of
Islam,* both sponsored by large university presses. Other projects are
under the auspices of organizations such as the United Nations, for
example, the UNESCO-sponsored *General History of Africa.* This is
an effective means of bringing to bear a degree of expertise that would
not be attainable if such vast projects were being undertaken by a single
author. There is also a significant saving of time involved, though large
joint projects have their own pitfalls, delays, and frustrations that sorely
test the skill and patience of general editors.

   Whether scholarly monographs or survey texts, all books have struc-
tural similarities that are important to note, especially when you are
trying to determine quickly the approach, interpretation, and scope of
a particular volume. These matters will be discussed in more detail in
Chapter 4, but a few pointers are in order here. A book's title will
usually be descriptive of its scope, but the subtitle (if there is one) will
tell you more. Recall the psychobiography of Jefferson by Fawn Brodie
discussed in Chapter 1. The title itself, *Thomas Jefferson,* reveals nothing more than that it is a biography. But the subtitle, *An Intimate
History,* gives a strong clue that this is not a standard political biography
of Jefferson the public figure. By looking at the chapter headings in the
Table of Contents and reading the Introduction, the kind of work one
is dealing with becomes clear. If these parts of the book help to determine the scope and approach of a book, the Index at the back allows
the book to be mined efficiently for information.

## Essays

An essay is a short, self-contained study, usually combined with similar
works in book form, though it might be published separately as a
pamphlet. It can be narrow or broad in scope, based on primary or
secondary sources, chiefly narrative or assertively interpretive. The essay
is a versatile, effective literary form for historians, as it is for scholars
in the other humanities. Usually, essays by different authors on the same

general topic or field are combined into a single work with a title such as *Essays in Business History*. The range of essays in such a volume might be very wide, for example, from an analysis of merchant enterprise in fourteenth-century Florence to a study of the advent of high-tech industries in California.

Sometimes the essays will have been published previously, perhaps in a different form, such as an article in a scholarly journal. The earlier articles and essays of eminent historians will often be gathered together and published. Or each member of a group of historians who were trained by the same scholar will contribute an essay to a book published in that person's honor, sometimes on the occasion of his or her retirement. Such a collection is called a *Festschrift*, a German word meaning a presentation volume of essays dedicated to someone.[1]

## Articles

Similar to essays in structure, length, and purpose, scholarly articles are an even more important segment of the body of secondary works. Articles are often the format in which historians first launch new and controversial interpretations. The process of revisionism would be greatly retarded if this mode of presenting historical findings and analyses were not available. For the student researcher, to ignore articles and confine one's attention to the available books would be to miss much of the freshest and most provocative literature on the subject. An appreciation of this large, diverse body of scholarship requires some understanding of the journals in which articles appear. This in turn will lead us to a consideration of the structure of the historical profession itself.

Usually, a periodical publication in which scholarly articles are published is called a journal. The term "magazine" should, for the most part, be confined to those periodicals of a more popular bent such as *Newsweek* or *The Atlantic Monthly*. There are a few historical periodicals, such as the British publication *History Today,* that have a popular magazine format, with short, amply illustrated articles designed for a wider readership. For the most part, however, historical journals

---

[1]An example is *Ideas and Institutions of Victorian Britain. Essays in Honour of George Kitson Clark*, ed. Robert Robson (London: Bell & Sons, 1967). The title of this book gives no clue to the specialized essays it contains. For this reason, essays are sometimes called the "hidden literature." How to find this "hidden literature" will be discussed in the next chapter.

are designed for a professional readership and feature lengthy, detailed articles, some of which can be daunting to a nonspecialist. This should not intimidate the undergraduate researcher; a history student who is properly launched on a particular topic should find most of the articles on that topic both readable and stimulating.

Many historical journals are published by associations of historians, with the costs of publication covered in part by membership subscriptions. In the United States, one of the leading historical journals is *The American Historical Review*, official organ of the American Historical Association. The AHA is the major "umbrella" organization for historians in the country; its thousands of members have every conceivable specialization and field of interest. Accordingly, the *American Historical Review* does not specialize in any field. In each of its five issues per year, there might be articles on modern Europe, Tang Dynasty China, Hellenistic Egypt, or colonial America. Methodologically, all approaches to the past are represented. Similarly, the hundreds of pages of book reviews that appear in each issue of this journal cover books in all fields of history. Book reviews play a vitally important role in the evaluation and analysis of historical works. They are part of the elaborate apparatus by which new views in history are submitted to close critical scrutiny.

*The American Historical Review* is notable not just for its size and importance, but also because it is atypical of historical journals. The great majority have some kind of focus or specialization. For example, *The Journal of American History* is published by the Organization of American Historians, whose members' primary interest is the history of the United States. This journal, as its name suggests, does not publish articles or book reviews outside the field of American history. The scope of many journals is defined by their titles: *The Journal of Modern History*, *The Journal of African Studies*, *The Journal of Contemporary History*, and *Byzantine Studies*. Some specialize not in time periods or geographic areas, but methodological approaches: *The Journal of Social History* or *The International Journal of Psychohistory*. Most are produced under the auspices of some professional organization. The North American Conference on British Studies, for example, supports the publication of two—*Albion* and *The Journal of British Studies*.

Many have a much narrower focus than this. Journals of local history are a prime example. In the United States, there is a great abundance of such publications. State historical societies and many societies devoted to the history of small localities publish their own journals. Researchers ignore these periodicals at their peril. Many important revisionist interpretations are produced in the form of article-length studies in local history journals.

Local studies are not only important in themselves; they offer a valuable means of validating or refuting general historical hypotheses. Any assertion about a society's characteristics can be tested by examining particular localities in great detail. If, for example, it is claimed that there was a high degree of social mobility in nineteenth-century America, how does this assertion stand up to examining social mobility from generation to generation? Since attempting to answer this question involves the analysis of massive amounts of occupational data from the Census as well as other material, a local study is the most feasible procedure. No single study could sustain or overturn the hypothesis, but a number of investigations could, and these sometimes are published in journals of state or local history.

## Dissertations and Conference Papers

Turning from those secondary sources readily accessible in published form, as books, essays, or articles, the student should consider two other forms in which new findings are presented—dissertations and conference papers.

A Ph.D. is the highest academic degree in history, and its completion requires the writing of a scholarly dissertation, usually on a rather narrow topic and based on intensive research in the primary sources. The granting of a Ph.D. in history follows the certifying by a committee of historians that the candidate's dissertation meets the standards of the profession. A dissertation is expected to demonstrate its author's critical acumen, writing abilities, and knowledge of the relevant primary and secondary sources. Dissertations are also usually expected to offer original analyses and interpretations. They can therefore be important works of revisionist scholarship in their own right. Some will be printed as books. Others will be substantially revised before ultimately being published or will eventually appear as journal articles. Even in their unrevised form, recent dissertations can be important tools for reseachers. Not only do they offer new interpretations, but their bibliographies are apt to be especially complete and are therefore excellent guides to the sources.[2]

Conference papers, delivered by historians to their peers at scholarly conferences, might be described as the "cutting edge" of revisionism. In many cases, this is the initial form in which the results of a historian's findings are made public and subjected to scrutiny and criticism. Often the criticism and discussion offered at a conference will guide the historian in revising his or her work before submitting it for publication. Typically, a conference paper will be presented as part of a panel containing two or three papers on similar topics. After an introduction by the scholar chairing the panel, each paper will be presented. After the papers have been read (each requiring perhaps 20 to 30 minutes), a commentary on the papers is given by a scholarly expert in the field. The commentator offers criticism, advice, and often the delineation of some themes or threads tying the papers together. The audience is then free to question, challenge, refine, and offer counter-interpretations. This can be a highly stimulating, even acrimonious exchange, but it is one of the principal means by which new views are expressed and modified prior to publication.

To get some idea of how this process operates, consider the largest historical conference of them all—the annual meeting of the American Historical Association. Held over a four-day period at the end of each December, the annual AHA meeting is a vast smorgasbord of offerings, with clusters of panels running simultaneously. At the 1986 meeting in Chicago, for example, there were no fewer than 123 panels on everything from "The Strange Career of Jim Crow Revisited" to "Millenarianism in Western History" to "The Enlightenment in Eastern Europe: The Romanian Case."[3] Each of the panels tends to attract for its audience specialists in the particular field, though many participants find

---

[2]A bound copy of each dissertation is available in the library of the university granting the Ph.D., but it does not usually circulate on Interlibrary Loan. Dissertations are available in microfilm and can be purchased from University Microfilms. It should be noted that many of the sources the student will use in research are in microform. Back issues of journals and newspapers, for example, are most often on reels of microfilm or sheets of microfiche. More and more primary sources are available in microform. Indeed, whole vast collections of manuscripts, rare pamphlets, books, government documents, and the like, are becoming available in microfiche.

[3]*American Historical Association. Program of the One Hundred First Annual Meeting* (Washington, D.C.: American Historical Association, 1986).

it stimulating to attend at least a few panels well outside their areas of primary interest.

In addition to the panels, the annual meeting is an occasion for publishers of scholarly books in history to display their wares. This is an important source of information for historians about the latest publications in the field. There are also numerous opportunities for social and intellectual exchanges during conferences—individual encounters, receptions, and the luncheons of the many historical societies affiliated to the AHA. It is these affiliated societies that are apt to be the primary focus of most historians' professional involvement. Many if not most of these also hold their own regular meetings and conferences independently of the AHA meeting. Like the specialized journals that cater to particular fields, the hundreds of historical societies are organized on geographic, cultural, chronological, or methodological bases. Such groups as the Society for Reformation Research, the American Conference on Irish Studies, the Society for the History of Technology, and the American Society for Environmental History represent a crucial part of the infrastructure of the historical profession.

This account of the basic organizational features of the profession is introduced in order to give some sense of the dynamic and cooperative character of modern scholarship. Most books and articles the student will encounter were not written by "ivory tower" types working in complete isolation but by men and women developing and refining their views in relation to the methods and criticisms of others. This is what is meant when the historical profession, or some segment of it, is described as a "community of scholars." In the next chapter the various methods of finding the works produced by those scholars who have written on a particular topic will be explored.

# 3

## Finding Sources: The Library Catalog and Beyond

A CHILD who asks for an item of general information will often be told to "look it up." This response, though it may proceed from the parent's unwillingness to admit ignorance, is an educationally sound one. Its tendency is to make the child a self-directed learner and to develop basic research skills. A children's encyclopedia or a "book of knowledge" may be the extent of the materials available in the home, but the lesson imparted is invaluable—that a storehouse of accumulated information is literally at one's fingertips. Beyond the home, the maturing student discovers the richer offerings of community and school libraries, which open up additional layers of knowledge and nourish the spirit of inquiry. Admission to college brings with it the highest stage of access to the written word in the form of the university library, the resources of which are usually much more voluminous and varied than anything encountered before.

In spite of the impressiveness of most campus libraries, however, many students remain unaware of the great diversity of materials and services they offer. Typical written assignments, such as term papers and book reviews, rarely require anything more than a few books from the library stacks. The procedure is simple and straightforward. Find some titles in the library catalog, jot down the call numbers, look them up, and check them out. At home, the selected volumes can be mined for information, including perhaps a few choice quotations. If additional material on a particular person or historical incident is needed, one of the large and authoritative encyclopedias in the reference room can be consulted. Having filled up some note cards or notebooks during this process, the student uses them to write the paper. The library can then be ignored (except as a refuge of more or less quiet study) until the next such assignment.

The procedure just outlined may serve well enough for the requirements of most lower-division survey courses. Its shortcomings become painfully obvious, however, as soon as more advanced coursework is encountered. A few of the more notable deficiencies of this time-honored method of undergraduate research should be considered. First, it is probably directed at only one or two of several subject headings under which books on the student's topic might be catalogued. Second, by confining itself to the books that the college library happens to possess, it ignores a vast and efficient Interlibrary Loan network that can obtain most published works on any topic for the student within a week or two. Third, this procedure makes no attempt to access scholarly journals, with their wealth of information and new interpretations. Fourth, it does not take into account an extraordinary richness of more specialized reference works that are highly useful. These deficiencies can be corrected by learning about the resources offered by several vital parts of the library often overlooked or underutilized by students—the Reference Room, the Periodicals Room, and the Interlibrary Loan office.

## The Library Catalog

Before examining these facilities, however, one should take another look at that part of the library students already know (or think they know)—the library catalog. If the reader is wondering why the more common term, "card catalog," is not used, it is because this resource is being transformed by the new technology. While the reassuring sight of the old card files still greets visitors to most libraries, computer terminals and microfiche readers are cropping up among the serried ranks of wooden drawers. All or most of a university library's holdings are now accessible by these new methods. In some cases, this operates in harness with the expansion of the old card file, each new acquisition being represented by a new card in the file as well as an entry in the computer's memory. In other cases, works acquired by the library after a certain date are catalogued *only* in the computer or on microfiche.

Whatever the exact system on each campus, the new technology, particularly the computerized catalog, offers numerous benefits to the user. With only a few minutes required to learn to use the terminal, the student can carry out a complete catalog search in a single location, instead of having to move around to perhaps dozens of drawers and rifle laboriously through hundreds of cards. Moreover, terminals are increasingly to be found in convenient locations throughout the library and other parts of the campus. In some cases it is even possible to carry out a catalog search from one's home, using a personal computer hooked up to a modem.

Whether one is looking at typewritten cards or at electronic characters on a screen, it is important to know the object of the search. The selection and refinement of your topic is of course a critical matter. It may be assigned by your instructor, but usually the student is expected to develop the topic, often within some defined parameters. Consultation with your instructor regarding the feasibility of your topic is always a good idea, but it should be realized that the topic will probably change during the course of your research. Usually this will be in the direction of limiting or pruning, since the original topic will be found to be overly broad. If, for example, your first idea was to write about nineteenth-century imperialism, you would have quickly discovered (or been told) that it was far too vast a subject. Seeking to limit it, you might have chosen British imperialism, German imperialism, or perhaps the "Scramble for Africa." These topics also proving unmanageable, you might have tried narrowing chronologically, geographically, or topically: for example, "German involvement in East Africa, 1884–1898," or "Cecil Rhodes and the expansion of the British Empire in South Africa, 1890–1902." To delimit the topic in this fashion requires that you already know something about imperialism or that you start your research by reading some general work on the subject.

## Subject Headings

The titles in the library catalog are arranged under three categories: author, title, and subject. You may start your research knowing about certain works from your instructor or from references encountered in textbooks. The author or title entries will provide the call numbers for these works, and the volumes can be garnered from the stacks, assuming of course that they are part of the library's holdings. But it is the subject entries that will probably engage you for most of your catalog search, and these require more care and thought. Under what subject headings should you look? Several subject headings, perhaps as many as a dozen, will yield useful titles, and it is up to you to determine which words or phrases to look under. This is where it becomes important to spend some time analyzing your topic, thinking about the various subjects of which it forms a part. After all, very few of the books in your final bibliography will be exactly on that topic.

Fortunately, the determination of subject headings is not entirely a matter of guesswork. After spending a few minutes thinking about and jotting down some possible subject headings, you can consult *Library of Congress Subject Headings,* a two-volume reference work (plus supplements) usually found in close proximity to the library catalog. This will allow you to discover what exact subject headings have been established in the classification system and what the call number ranges are for the major headings. Armed with this information you can then go to the subject entries in the catalog to continue the search.

You will almost certainly be looking through a rather disparate range of subject headings. If your topic is German imperialism in Africa, for example, a couple of the useful subject headings turn out to be "Germany—Colonies—Africa" and "Germany—Colonies—History." As you begin to read some of the books on this topic, you may return to the subject catalog to search under the heading "Peters, Karl." This refers to the intrepid German explorer and empire-builder whose career bulks as large in the history of German East Africa as that of Cecil Rhodes does in the history of British South Africa. It is an example of how a number of topics turn out to have significant biographical components. Important information on your topic would thus be found in a biography of Peters. The reverse is also true. Having a biographical topic such as Cecil Rhodes might seem to simplify the process: just copy down the entries under "Rhodes, Cecil" and you're through. But here too there will be a number of headings to look under. Important information on Rhodes is contained in studies of South Africa in the late nineteenth century, histories of Rhodesia, and accounts of the Boer War.

You may be wondering if all this means that you must somehow manage to determine all the subject headings for your topic in order to get a complete bibliography. The answer is no. Library cataloguers, in their infinite wisdom and mercy, have devised a useful system of cross-referencing, notably the "tracings" that appear on each entry in the library catalog. Let us say that you had begun to research the history of women in the United States. You would have learned from the

*Library of Congress Subject Headings* that one of the headings to use is "Women—United States—History." Going to this heading in the catalog, you would find a number of potentially useful titles, including one that was encountered in the first chapter—June Sochen's *Herstory*. The bibliographic information for this book in the catalog (omitting some material not essential for our purposes) is:

---

WOMEN—UNITED STATES—HISTORY

HQ        Sochen, June, 1937–
1410      Herstory: a woman's view of American history/
S64       June Sochen. New York: Alfred Pub. Co., [1974]
          xiii, 448p. : ill. ; 24cm.

          Includes bibliographies and index.
          ISBN 0-88284-017-7
          ISBN 0-88284-018-5 pbk.

          1. Women—United States—History.
          2. Women—United States—Social Conditions.
          3. United States—Social Conditions.
          4. Minorities—United States.

---

In addition to the title, author, call number, date, place, and publisher, the reader is given other basic information: the book has a 13-page preface (note the Roman numeral xiii), has 448 pages of text, and contains illustrations (note the "ill."), a bibliography, and an index. The second ISBN (International Standard Book Number) tells the reader that there is or was a paperback edition (note the "pbk."). But it is the tracings that are our chief concern. These are the four subject headings listed at the bottom of the card. The first of them also appears in capital letters at the top and is the heading that was used to find this particular card. The other three tracings are headings under which Sochen's book can also be located, along with other works likely to be of interest. Get into the habit of jotting down the other tracings (sometimes there is only one) from each subject catalog entry you look up.

## Keeping a Bibliography Card File

Another important habit to acquire early in the game is developing complete bibliography cards on all entries that are obviously or potentially of use. Use 3 × 5 cards, of one color for secondary works and of another for primary sources. Write the author's or editor's name on the top line (last name first) with the title, publication data, and call number below. As the card files are built up (separate ones for primary and secondary sources), keep the entries alphabetized so that you can tell at a glance if there is already a card on a particular book. This will also make it easy when the paper is finished and it is time to type the bibliography. It is also useful to make other notations on the bibliography cards. For example, a mark next to the call number can show the library where the book was found. A check mark in one corner can indicate if you have already read the book or at least looked at it; brief annotations on its contents will prove helpful.

Once you are launched on your project, always take your card file and a supply of blank cards with you to the library. As you access the stacks using the catalog, new titles will loom into view frequently. One of the ways this happens may already be familiar—it is called "shelf browsing." This entails simply examining the volumes adjacent to those books you have gone to the stacks to fetch—some of them are almost certain to prove valuable. Disdained by purists as an amateurish method, it is nonetheless highly effective. Another important method, untainted by any hint of amateurishness, is mining the bibliographies of the books found. One of the advantages of this method is that it will lead you to the titles of works that the library does not have in its holdings; they can then be obtained through Interlibrary Loan or by going to another library.

## Published Bibliographies

Another very effective means of finding titles is to consult published bibliographies available in book, article, or essay form. It may indeed be advisable to begin the search in this fashion. Discussing this resource has been deferred until now because it is essential to start with some knowledge of the organization of the library catalog, particularly the subject catalog. Also, finding a published bibliography on one's topic

at the outset might tend to short circuit the search and thus interfere
with learning some basic research procedures. In addition to those
scholars who write histories or edit primary source materials, others
provide a most valuable service by collecting and publishing bibliographies on various subjects. These are intended as guides to researchers
and provide a list of books and articles on the subject, often arranged
under subtopics and sometimes annotated. Annotations are the editor's
comments and indicate something about the scope and usefulness of
each entry. When these research guides are written as essays rather than
simply lists of titles they are called bibliographic essays.

Bibliographies can be located in a number of ways. The subject index
of the catalog is one method. When you have discovered an appropriate
heading for the topic, look at the heading immediately following it to
see if there is one with the word "Bibliography" added. It will be
recalled that for research on the history of American women one of
the key headings is "Women—United States—History." Immediately
following the cards in this category in the subject index is the heading
"Women—United States—History—Bibliography." Here will be found
the titles of a number of valuable bibliographies on this topic or some
portion of it. An example is Jill K. Conway, *The Female Experience in
Eighteenth and Nineteenth Century America: A Guide to the History
of American Women* (New York: Garland Pub., 1982). In Conway's
bibliography will be found the titles of thousands of books, articles,
and collections of primary sources on various facets of the history of
American women. It is a good idea whenever looking up something in
the subject catalog to see if there is also a bibliography heading for the
topic. The same holds true for primary sources. If there are published
sources for the topic in the library there will be a heading in the subject
index with the word "Sources" added. One should look, for example,
under the heading "Women—United States—History—Sources."

In the Reference Room of the library are other ways to access bibliographies. There are several good "bibliographies of bibliographies,"
which list bibliographies in all fields. A particularly good one for historical researchers is Eugene P. Sheehy, *Guide to Reference Books,* 10th
ed. (Chicago and London: American Library Association, 1986), a work
that is regularly revised and updated. By looking up the entries under
history and the appropriate subheading, you will find references to
bibliographic works on your topic or on that field of history of which
your topic is a part. For example, if the topic is in the history of the

United States, the Sheehy volume will direct you to the *Harvard Guide to American History,* an excellent two-volume bibliography. Each time you find a useful published bibliography like this, be sure to make out a bibliography card—preferably of a color different from those used for primary and secondary sources.

While you are in the Reference Room, also have a look at the latest issues of the *Bibliographic Index.* You may well need different subject headings for this and other indexes you will use, but the principle will be the same. In this particular index, you will find the titles of bibliographic essays and articles in scholarly journals as well as books. Besides guiding you to bibliographic works, the *Bibliographic Index* will direct you to histories of the topic that have bibliographies. Since most scholarly books include bibliographies, this is another excellent way to find titles of secondary works not in your library.

Another method of finding relevant titles the library may not have is to consult the subject index of *Books in Print,* a multivolume reference work that is frequently updated. A few weeks after you first examine the *Bibliographic Index* and *Books in Print,* you should return to the Reference Room to check the latest supplements. In this way you will be able to stay reasonably current with the latest scholarship on your topic, although there is necessarily a time lag between the publication of a book and its appearance in any of the reference sources. This practice of returning to the Reference Room to examine the latest supplements applies as well to the other indexes and abstracts that will now be considered—those that provide access to articles in scholarly journals and essays in books.

## Indexes to Periodical Literature

In the last chapter the importance of scholarly journals in the process of historical revisionism was seen. Scholarly articles are not mere adjuncts to books; they are efficient vehicles for presenting various kinds of special studies as well as the initial form in which historians often challenge existing interpretations. It is therefore vitally important to find and read the relevant periodical literature. There are several indexing and abstracting resources available for this purpose. Most of them are published quarterly and are bound into volumes at the end of each year with a comprehensive index. Some provide five- or ten-year indexes to facilitate the search. When you first consult each of these reference works, spend a few minutes acquainting yourself with the internal organization and seeing which subject headings are used for the topic. Start with the most recently published supplement and work backward in time. How far back one goes depends on the topic, the kind of paper, and the guidelines set by the instructor.

Many students will already be somewhat familiar with the *Readers' Guide to Periodical Literature*. This widely used reference work is a good index to popular publications, but a glance at the list of magazines at the front of any volume of the *Readers' Guide* reveals very few scholarly journals. Accessing articles on the topics that appear in the vast majority of the historical journals requires indexes that are more specialized and scholarly. A good starting point is the *Humanities Index*, which indexes most of the major English language historical journals. Before 1974, this index was part of the *Social Science and Humanities Index*. Be sure to make a card for each article including all the essential bibliographic information—author, title, name of journal, volume, date, and page numbers. If for example, the topic is the domestic policies of Louis XIV, you would find a reference to a useful article in *The Historian* and should fill out a card as follows:

---

Riley, Philip E.

"Louis XIV: Watchdog of Parisian Morality,"

The Historian 36 (November 1973): 19-33.

---

Since the example used here is of a biographical topic, it would be rewarding to consult another valuable reference source called the *Biography Index*. Remember that whether the topic concerns a single individual or not, it may have a significant biographical component.

Thus a paper on American naval expansion in the 1890s will necessarily give considerable space to the activities of Theodore Roosevelt; one on the rise of anticolonialism in India in the twentieth century could hardly ignore Gandhi; a study of Athenian imperialism will almost certainly be concerned with the policies of Pericles. The *Biography Index* will therefore be of use for a great many topics. Furthermore, this index directs you to books and essays as well as to scholarly journal articles.

## Abstracts of Historical Articles

The indexes that have been examined are vital and indispensable, but they do not provide anything beyond titles, authors, and bibliographic citations. From this basic information you must try to determine whether a particular article is necessary. If the journal is part of the library's holdings, this may pose no particular problem. But what if it is not, and you want to know whether it is worth the bother (and possible expense) of getting a copy of the article through Interlibrary Loan? Here is where abstracts prove their value. Abstracts are organized like indexes but they provide more information—after each entry there is a description of the scope and contents of the article. This does not mean you can ignore the indexes and go straight to the abstracts. A somewhat different range of scholarly journals are covered by the abstracts, and the most widely available set of abstracts for European history covers only the Renaissance to the present. If your topic was in ancient or medieval history, you would not find a thing. Even for modern history you would miss some important articles, since some of the journals covered in the indexes are not covered by the abstracts. These are some of the quirks in the organization of the materials for historical research.

   The two most important abstracts for our purposes are *Historical Abstracts* and *America: History and Life.* The first is for European and world history from the Renaissance to the present, while the latter is concerned with American history. The structure and arrangement of abstracts are a little different from indexes, so one must spend a little time becoming oriented before commencing the search. It will be noticed that each of the abstracts is organized into several parts, including article abstracts and citations, an index to book reviews, a bibliography of books, articles, and dissertations, and an annual index. The subject headings will be found to be different from those encountered so far, because they refer exclusively to historical materials. Thus, for example, no heading with "History" appended to it will be found. Nor will "United States" be added to any subject heading in *America: History and Life.*

Also notice how very different are the journals listed in the abstracts from those covered by the indexes. It is a much longer list and includes many journals of local history. In *America: History and Life,* for example, there are a very large number of publications dealing with state and local history, such as the *Utah Historical Quarterly,* the *Pennsylvania Magazine of Biography and History,* the *Southern California Quarterly,* and *Chicago History.* One might think that these journals would be of little use unless the topic happened to be concerned with the state or city in question. But remember in the discussion of secondary works in the last chapter that important revisionist scholarship often appears in the form of local studies.

Thus if you were writing about the Freedmen's Bureau, that subject heading in Vol. 17 of *America: History and Life* would lead you to the title and abstract of an article by James Stealey in the journal *West Virginia History* with the title of "The Freedmen's Bureau in West Virginia":

> 17 A: 1135. Stealey, James Edmund III. THE FREEDMEN'S BUREAU IN WEST VIRGINIA. West Virginia History 1978 39(2–3): 99–142. During 1865–68 the Freedmen's Bureau was active in Berkeley and Jefferson counties, West Virginia, where freedmen were a fifth of the population. The young army officers in charge were zealous for the blacks' welfare but did not have much success in protecting their legal rights. The establishment of schools met a mixed white reception, especially where the black attendance was large; the Bureau's most significant effort was in the founding of Storer College, a Negro normal school. Based on Freedmen's Bureau records and other primary and secondary sources; 216 notes.
>
> J. H. Broussard

The information provided here will help you decide whether to add this title to the bibliography. It sounds quite useful, and if your paper were on the educational activities of the Freedmen's Bureau, you almost certainly would want it. Note also that this is quite a lengthy article based on research in the primary sources and has a large number of footnotes or endnotes. J. H. Broussard wrote the abstract. If you decide to use it, fill out a bibliography card and submit an Interlibrary Loan request (unless, of course, your library has *West Virginia History* in its holdings).

## Finding Scholarly Essays

The procedures just described should guide you efficiently to the articles in scholarly journals. But how does one find the scholarly essays that appear in books with titles that give little or no clue to the specialized nature of the essays they contain? This is the problem of the "hidden literature" referred to in Chapter 2. The answer is to consult that indispensable reference source, the *Essay and General Literature Index*. Organized like the other indexes, it provides access to the titles of essays that appear in books. For example, if your topic were the economic aspect of decolonization in Africa, you would find under the subject heading "Africa" in Vol. 10 of the *Essay and General Literature Index* a reference to an essay by Jean Suret-Canale titled "From Colonization to Independence in French Tropical Africa: The Economic Background," in a book with the title of *The Transfer of Power in Africa*. Deciding that this would be definitely useful, you should look up the book in the library catalog under the title or the name of one of the editors and proceed to fill out a bibliography card as follows:

> Suret-Canale, Jean
>
> "From colonialization to independence in french Tropical Africa: the economic background," in The Transfer of power in Africa: Decolonization, 1940-1960. Edited by Prosser Gifford and William Roger Louis. New Haven: Yale University Press, 1982. Pp. 445-481.

A thorough examination of the indexes and abstracts just described should yield most of the titles of important articles and essays on your topic. This does not mean that all of them, any more than all the books that were located, will find a place in the final bibliography. An essential pruning operation lies ahead, and this process will be discussed in the next chapter. There is one important thing to do with articles and essays, however, almost as soon as you begin reading them—mine their footnotes or endnotes for additional bibliographic references. This is identical to the procedure followed in mining the bibliographies of books and will ensure that few if any essential titles slip through the net.


## Bibliographic Search by Computer

As in the case of the library catalog, computer technology has made significant contributions to the more extended methods of bibliographic search just described. The major historical indexes and abstracts are available as on-line data bases and accessible to some degree by most university libraries. Ideally, this offers the prospect of a major saving of time compared to wading through each of the indexes and abstracts in the Reference Room. Seated at a console, the searcher could type in several subject headings and sit back as the computer quickly retrieved titles from the data bases and generated a printed bibliography. This ideal may some day be a reality, but for the present there are a number of flaws in this technological paradise.

To begin with, the data bases currently in use only cover the last few years of publication and are thus useless for retrieving any of the older titles. Second, access is often limited to certain hours and days, depending upon the contract between the library and the data base company. The company charges the library for each search, often on a time basis, and this charge is sometimes passed on wholly or partially to the searcher. This makes it very difficult to carry out a full search using various subject headings. Using the bound volumes in the Reference Room one can quickly check to see which subject headings are apt to pay off, but with an on-line system it is important to know the headings before commencing the search. It is of course possible to use a combination of the methods. For example, one could go first to the *Humanities Index* or *Historical Abstracts* and find the subject headings that lead to useful titles. These subject headings can then be used for an on-line search.

Computer-searching resources are apt to improve in the next few years, perhaps substantially. The greatest promise lies in the direction of replacing on-line systems with data bases on disks. This has already begun in some disciplines, and is now being extended to history. A disk-based system will remove many of the present disadvantages, such as limited accessibility and cost constraints for the library or the searcher. Also, as libraries acquire the new disk systems, the time-depth of the data base will increase with each advancing year, rendering it more and more useful for historical searchers. Obviously, the state of computer bibliographic searching is in flux, and major improvements are on the way. Whatever the system in your library, you should learn about it and avail yourself of all the assistance it affords.

The emphasis in this chapter has been on locating secondary works, with one brief aside about checking to see if there is a subject heading in the catalog for the topic with the word "Sources" added to it. If there were, you would be able to lay hands on some of the published collections of primary sources. There are other methods of locating primary source materials, but these will be discussed in Chapter 5, where the writing of a research paper based on them will be examined. The reason for emphasizing the finding of secondary sources here is that it is essential to have read some of the important studies by other historians before plunging into the primary sources. Furthermore, since in the next chapter the writing of a historiographic essay will be explored, secondary sources are now the chief concern. But before turning to that challenging task, it is necessary to consider some other things of great value the Reference Room offers.

## Other Riches of the Reference Room

Our chief concern with the Reference Room so far has been with the major indexes and abstracts. But these by no means exhaust the materials of interest to historical researchers. First of all, there are a number of more specialized indexes to periodical literature that may be of interest, depending on your topic. For any topic in British or European history, the *British Humanities Index* is apt to prove helpful. Those researching any aspect of the history of law will want to consult the *Index to Legal Periodicals*. The law journals indexed in the latter are, for the most part, not found in the other indexes. Some of the articles in law journals are of a historical character and are important vehicles for launching revisionist interpretations. Other indexes that may prove valuable to historical researchers are the *Art Index*, the *Music Index*, and *Index Medicus* (wherein, for example, might be found a reference to an article in a scientific journal on King George III's alleged insanity). There may also be some other useful abstracts in addition to the two major ones discussed earlier, such as *Dissertation Abstracts International*.

In addition to the valuable indexes and abstracts that have been discussed, there is a great diversity of materials of interest to historians, such as encyclopedias (both general and specialized), biographical dictionaries of every conceivable kind, atlases, almanacs, and official guides to various countries. Indexes to book reviews, such as the *Book Review Index* and the *Index to Book Reviews in Historical Periodicals,* are also likely to prove serviceable. The best procedure is to go on an exploratory journey around the Reference Room, armed with 3 × 5 cards, preferably of a color different from those employed for other kinds of sources.

It is important to determine the basic scheme of organization of the Reference Room, since there are important variations from library to library. In some, for example, all the atlases will be found together, whatever part of the world and time period they cover. Or all the biographical materials will be grouped together without regard to geographic region or historical era. Other libraries will aggregate their reference materials on much the same system as the books in the stacks. Often there will be a combination of these two systems. Once you understand the layout, you will quickly discover a number of valuable and often fascinating reference tools. As this is done, you should jot down the title and call number of each (or location in the Reference Room) on a card. One should not hesitate to ask the reference librarian for help—both in finding reference works and in using them.

Reference works can of course be located through the subject headings of the library catalog. But this is an area where "shelf browsing" is apt to be particularly effective, especially if the materials in the Reference Room have the same call number ranges as the books in the stacks dealing with the same topics. If your topic is some aspect of the Spanish Civil War, notice that many of the call numbers of the books you find start with DP (assuming that your library uses the Library of Congress classification system). DP is the classification for Spanish history. If you go to the DPs in the Reference Room, you will possibly discover a highly useful *Historical Dictionary of the Spanish Civil War, 1936–1939*.[1] This volume provides a wealth of information on the major and minor figures of that conflict, plus descriptions of major parties, campaigns, battles, and the like. There is a similar reference work on the Vietnam War, with entries for all the battles, campaigns, and persons involved, plus a detailed chronology of events.[2] Those working in ancient history will find the nearly 1,200 pages of entries in *The New Century Classical Handbook*[3] invaluable.

The foregoing examples are only a minute sample of the riches that await you in the Reference Room. Whatever kind of paper you are writing and whatever the topic, there are bound to be reference materials of vital importance. Used intelligently in harness with the primary and secondary sources, they will both deepen your understanding and lighten your labors. The contributions of the Reference Room should be kept in mind as we explore in the next two chapters the writing of a historiographic essay and a research paper.

---

[1] Edited by James W. Cortada (London: Greenwood Press, 1982).
[2] *The Vietnam War: An Almanac*. Edited by John S. Bowman, with an introduction by Fox Butterfield (New York: World Almanac Publications, 1985).
[3] Edited by Catherine B. Avery (New York: Appleton-Century-Croft, 1962).

# 4

## Exploring Changing Interpretations: The Historiographic Essay

IN THIS chapter the nature of the revisionist process will be explored more fully by considering the writing of a historiographic essay. In the first chapter we examined a few of the major currents of historiography in the broadest sense of the word—that is, the history of history writing. Our concern now will be with historiography in its narrower meaning— the variety of approaches, methods, and interpretations employed by historians on any given topic. The historiographic essay is an important literary form in its own right, providing the reader with a sense of how the topic he or she is interested in has already been approached by previous historians. An awareness of the historiography on your topic is an essential prerequisite to undertaking research and writing using primary sources. Knowing the kinds of approaches and interpretations already employed by others, as well as the still unanswered questions on the topic, can help direct your inquiry along original lines. The writing of a historiographic essay is also an excellent learning exercise, since in order to write one it is necessary to become immersed in the intellectual processes of historians as they modify and revise our view of the past.

### Selecting and Refining a Topic

Selecting and refining a topic is vitally important. Many students are inclined to choose a particularly vivid historical incident, such as the Japanese attack on Pearl Harbor or the assassination of Abraham Lincoln, in the belief that it will prove both interesting and manageable. In this they are not deceived. The intrinsic human drama of such events, as well as their being limited to short and specific spans of time, makes them attractive to the busy undergraduate. This is no doubt a major reason that some topic or other in military history is often a first choice. Another is that in many cases the survey courses students have encountered emphasize military conflicts and the more dramatic political events. Indeed, many of these are quite suitable subjects for a historiographic essay, since they have been approached and interpreted by historians in a variety of ways. But before seizing too readily on one of them, the student should ponder the many alternatives that are open.

Based upon what was learned in previous chapters of this book, other encounters with historiography, or the content of some of your history courses, you may wish to consider a less traditional topic—assuming, that is, that the instructor has not set precise guidelines or actually assigned a topic. For example, there is an abundance of fascinating subjects in social history, each with a rich and varied historiography. Numerous books, articles, and essays have been written on aspects of the history of education, sexuality, trade unions, sports, religion, immigration, popular entertainment, and crime. The history of science, technology, or industry can also provide viable and interesting topics. Selecting something like this may seem less familiar and comfortable than a more traditional topic, but it also offers greater opportunities for expanding intellectual horizons. Even if you choose a biographical topic, it need not concern a well-known political or military figure. Many thousands of fascinating men and women in all fields of endeavor throughout history have been the subject of significant scholarly attention.

The initial selection of a topic usually needs to be followed by a process of refining. Frequently the subject turns out to be too broad; occasionally it is too narrow. One would soon discover, for example, that a topic such as Renaissance humanism was extraordinarily vast and complex. It has such an extensive literature that it would not be possible to find, read, and analyze most of it within the time constraints of the course and the space limitations of the paper. The solution would be a drastic reduction of scope chronologically, geographically, topically, or biographically. A combination of these methods of narrowing is exemplified in a title such as "The Medici and Civic Humanism in Fifteenth Century Florence." Even this may require additional refinement, but clearly it is much more manageable than the first choice. The precise scope of one's paper probably will not be defined until one has gained some notion of the dimensions of the historiography.

## Research for a Historiographic Essay: A Case Study

The finding of historical sources was described in general terms in the last chapter; now the process as it applies to a specific topic will be examined. The example that will be considered is a fifteen-page paper (plus endnotes and bibliography) written by Yvette Berthel, a student in my History Methods class. It is titled "The American Social Settlement Movement, 1886–1914: A Historiographic Essay."[1] This paper serves well as an example, since it cuts across a number of important topics in American social history—education, religion, women, immigrants, progressivism, and urban history, to name a few. It also has important biographical dimensions, especially the vital role played in the movement by Jane Addams (1860–1935). Addams was the founder of Hull House in Chicago, arguably the most influential of the settlement houses in American cities that were patterned after Toynbee Hall in London. Settlement houses were established in poor urban areas and staffed by idealistic, well-educated members of the middle class, most of them women. Settlement workers sought to mitigate the problems facing the urban poor (many of them recent immigrants) not only by providing practical help and education but by living among them and thus offering an example of dedication, discipline, and hard work. The settlement movement was an important component of the powerful reforming impulse that swept through many areas of American life in the generation before World War I.

If you had chosen to write about the settlement movement, you probably already had some basic knowledge of the topic, including names that might prove fruitful as subject headings. "Addams, Jane" and "Hull House" are two examples. Or you might look in the subject headings of the library catalog under "Settlements." You would be referred from this heading to "Social Settlements," under which you would find several useful titles. One that would obviously be valuable, partly because it almost exactly coincides with the chronological dimensions of the paper, is Allen Freeman Davis, *Spearheads for Reform: The Social Settlements and the Progressive Movement, 1890–1914* (New York: Oxford University Press, 1967). A 3 × 5 bibliography card should be filled out for this volume.

---

[1] I wish to express my gratitude to Ms. Berthel, who has gone on to graduate study in history at the University of California, Santa Barbara, for permission to cite and quote at length from her paper. See pp. 49–55.

Although you are only at the beginning of the bibliographic search, it would be a good idea to get the Davis book from the stacks at once and begin reading it. This is because you need to acquire a great deal more factual knowledge of the topic in order to complete the search for titles. In reading it, you would be struck by the overwhelming preponderance of women in the movement, and this would lead you to search under various subtopics of American women's history. The same applies to religion, immigration, and the progressive movement. Also, if you recalled the use of tracings from the last chapter, you would have looked for these at the bottom of the catalog card for *Spearheads for Reform*. There you would have found that the book is cross-referenced under the subject headings "Progressivism (United States Politics)" and "Cities and Towns—United States." Looking under these headings may yield other books where the settlement movement is a large and important topic within a study of progressivism or urban history. Remember also to mine the bibliography in the Davis book for titles.

A variety of other subject headings also prove useful for this topic, including "United States—Social Conditions," "United States—Emigration and Immigration," and "Education of Women—United States— Biography." It is pointless to pursue this discussion of the library catalog search far beyond this point, since you would quickly be discovering titles by other means—bibliographies and footnotes of books and articles, published bibliographical essays and books, reference sources such as *Books in Print*, and good old shelf browsing. After exploring these various avenues, you should come up with the following list of books in addition to the Davis volume and proceed to fill out bibliography cards for each of them:

Addams, Jane. *Philanthropy and Social Progress*. Montclair, N. J.: Patterson Smith, 1970.

Lagemann, Ellen Condliffe. *A Generation of Women: Education in the Lives of Progressive Reformers*. Cambridge, Mass.: Harvard University Press, 1979.

Lasch, Christopher. *The New Radicalism in America 1889–1963*. New York: Alfred A. Knopf, 1965.

Levine, Daniel. *Varieties of Reform Thought*. Madison, Wis.: State Historical Society of Wisconsin, 1964.

McBride, Paul. *Culture Clash: Immigrants and Reformers. 1880–1920.*
San Francisco: R & E Research Associates, 1975.
O'Neill, William L. *Everyone Was Brave: The Rise and Fall of Feminism in America.* Chicago: Quadrangle Books, 1969.
Woods, Robert A., and Albert J. Kennedy. *The Settlement Horizon.*
New York: Arno Press, 1970.

The first and the last books might seem out of place, since, as essays and addresses by persons who were participants in the settlement movement, they are primary rather than secondary sources. But it is perfectly acceptable, sometimes even necessary, to use certain primary sources in a historiographic essay, especially when they are autobiographical, or of a reflective or interpretive character. Concerning the remainder, which are all secondary works, it should be realized that this is by no means a complete list of the scholarly books on the topic. Many important local studies and some general studies are left out. The chief criterion in making the selection, beyond the appearance of scholarly competence, is to achieve a variety of approaches to and interpretations of the subject.

A glance at the titles indicates the variety of approaches the authors have taken. Some have treated the settlement movement as an aspect of philanthropy, others see it as part of the reform movement, or a component of turn-of-the-century feminism. Some of the authors focus on the importance of the movement in the lives of women settlement workers, while others are interested in the impact of it on immigrants. These are only some of the basic differences evident from a cursory glance at titles and tables of contents. Many more differences will become apparent when the books are read and analyzed.

In the search for scholarly articles on this topic the abstracts in *America: History and Life* prove valuable, as well as the listings in the *Humanities Index* and the *Social Sciences Index*. Headings such as "Social Settlements" and "Addams, Jane" yield some important articles, including the following:

Conway, Jill. "Women Reformers and American Culture, 1870–1930."
*Journal of Social History* 5 (1971–72): 164–77.
Dougherty, James. "Jane Addams: Culture and Imagination." *Yale Review* 71 (Spring 1982): 363–79.

Greenstone, J. David. "Dorothea Dix and Jane Addams; from Transcendentalism to Pragmatism in American Social Reform." *Social Service Review* 53 (December 1979): 527–59.

Reinders, Robert C. "Toynbee Hall and the American Settlement Movement." *Social Service Review* 56 (1982): 39–54.

As in the case of the book titles, this is by no means an exhaustive list, but it does provide a range of approaches. The Reinders article, for example, obviously explores the question of the similarities between the American and British settlement houses. Greenstone places the career of Jane Addams in perspective by comparing it with that of the earlier reformer Dorothea Dix (1802–1887). Conway places the role of women in the settlement movement in the context of sixty years of involvement by women in a variety of reform movements. Again, these differences among the approaches taken by the authors are evident simply from the titles. A bibliography card should be filled out for each.

Turning to the essays or "hidden literature," we are well served by the *Essay and General Literature Index*. The same subject headings that proved successful in the search for books and articles yield the titles of four recent essays, each of which must be entered on a bibliography card:

Cook, Blanche Wiessen. "Female Support Networks and Political Activism: Lillian Wald, Crystal Eastman, Emma Goldman." In *A Heritage of Her Own: Toward a New Social History of American Women,* pp. 412–44. Edited by Nancy F. Cott and Elizabeth H. Pleck. New York: Simon and Schuster, 1979.

Gifford, Carolyn DeSwarte. "Women in Social Reform Movements." In *Women and Religion in America,* Vol. 1, *The Nineteenth Century,* pp. 294–340. Edited by Rosemary Radford Ruether and Rosemary Skinner Keller. San Francisco: Harper and Row, 1981.

Keller, Rosemary Skinner. "Lay Women in the Protestant Tradition." In *Women and Religion in America,* Vol. 1, *The Nineteenth Century,* pp. 242–93. Edited by Rosemary Radford Ruether and Rosemary Skinner Keller. San Francisco: Harper and Row, 1981.

Rousmaniere, John P. "Cultural Hybrid in the Slums: The College Woman and the Settlement House, 1889–1894." In *Women's*

*Experience in America,* pp. 169–92. Edited by Esther Katz and
Anita Rapone. New Brunswick, N.J.: Transaction Books, 1980.

Once again the titles are instructive, but note that in a couple of cases
it is necessary to take the title of the book in which the essay appears
into account as well. "Women in Social Reform Movements" is an
example. That it appears in a volume titled *Women and Religion in
America* provides the additional clue that the author examines the
religious motivation of women in the settlement movement. It might
be noted in passing that though many of the recent works on the subject
involve some aspect of women's history, they embody a great range of
differing perspectives.

Having a good array of books, articles, and essays that incorporate
a variety of different approaches to the topic, you might consider the
bibliography to be sufficient to the purpose at hand. Still, you might
wonder if there are any recent dissertations that would prove valuable.
A search through *Dissertation Abstracts International* turns up a 1981
Ph.D. dissertation from the University of Texas by Elizabeth Palmer
Hutcheson Carrell entitled "Reflections in a Mirror: The Progressive
Woman and the Settlement Experience." It sounds interesting and important. Remember, too, that dissertations usually have very complete
bibliographies. Whether to go ahead and order it will depend on your
instructor's opinion as well as the time at your disposal since it will
usually take a couple of weeks or more to get the microfilm or pho-
tocopy. Expense will be an additional consideration. But if it proves
feasible, you would be well advised to obtain any recent dissertation
on your topic.

## Writing the Historiographic Essay

We can now turn to the writing of a historiographic essay on this
subject. It is important to remember that this is not a history of the
settlement movement, but rather an account of how historians have
written about the settlement movement. Of course, a number of facts
concerning social settlements in America will be introduced into the
essay, but they are used to illustrate the approaches and findings of the
various authors. A good method is to think of oneself as preparing a
guide to the historiography for a fellow student who knows something

about the period but has a very limited knowledge of the topic. The introduction to the paper can therefore set forth some facts about the settlement movement to remind or inform the reader of some basic features of the topic. Consider the opening paragraph in Yvette Berthel's historiographic essay:

> In January, 1885, Toynbee Hall opened its doors to the poor people of London. Staffed by resident male university graduates, Toynbee Hall influenced the movement to establish social settlement houses in America. Located in areas inhabited by new immigrants and urban blacks, American settlement houses opened throughout the country, but were most highly concentrated in the densely-populated industrial centers of the northeast and midwest. New York's Neighborhood Guild, established in 1886, became the first of these houses which provided a variety of services, programs, and social clubs for the urban poor. While in 1891 there were only six settlements in America, by 1897 there were seventy-four, and by 1910 there were four hundred, the movement having reached its peak on the eve of World War I.

After some additional introductory material, Ms. Berthel gets to the body of her essay, starting with the interpretation of the settlement movement offered by Jane Addams and other participants in it. In the extended selection that follows, note how the author moves on from Addams and others to the newer kinds of interpretations offered by historians. Footnotes have been omitted so as not to impede the text. In her essay, the author properly included a footnote reference to each of the points she made respecting the various works in her bibliography. The authors to whom she refers in the following passage are those listed in the preceding pages.

> The traditional interpretation of the American settlement movement suggests that the movement sprang from an impulse founded in Christian humanitarianism and the desire of some people to make the world a better place in which to live. This interpretation is found in early twentieth century authors including Jane Addams, Robert Woods, and Albert Kennedy. It suggests that the atmosphere of the day was one of fervid philanthropy, genuine Christian piety, and a reform-minded attitude toward socializing democracy. In a word, it was the brainchild of a group of progressive reformers.
>
> A more modern interpretation is found in the writings of historians who focus on the movement's religious roots. In a book published in 1967, Allen Freeman Davis suggests that the mainstream of settlement resident

workers were Congregationalists and Presbyterians charged with a sense
of mission and personal responsibility to solve the world's problems. J.
David Greenstone supports Davis's opinion by commenting on the powerful thrust of Calvinist theology which pushed settlement workers to
prove themselves morally rather than economically. Yet Greenstone also
considers the atmosphere of the day to have been marked by a transition
from what he describes as an era of moral certainty and self-reliance to
one of collective action and moral inquiry. This transition is emphasized
by Christopher Lasch, who maintains that it was the waning of theology
rather than the persistence of piety that created the climate out of which
the American settlements emerged.

In attempting to determine who comprised the majority of resident
workers, certain historians have taken up the role of Protestant women
in American settlement work. Rosemary Skinner Keller points to the influx
of large numbers of Protestant deaconesses into evangelical organizations
in the late nineteenth century. This influx, she notes, was punctuated by
the entrance of such women into settlement houses for the purposes of
evangelism and conversion among new immigrants. Usually single women
and the daughters of ministers or of women's society leaders, Protestant
deaconesses were the pioneers of settlement work, according to Keller.
She stresses that the settlement houses not only benefited the prospective
convert through education and medical attention, but benefited the evan-
gelizing women by showing them a way in which they might organize
themselves outside of their traditional roles as wives and mothers. Carolyn
DeSwarte Gifford takes up this point and relates the women's new-found
sense of power and control, not only to the work being done in settlements, but to that being done in temperance and women's rights movements.

Elizabeth Carrell also points to the importance of the religious impulse
in the work of women resident workers, but she ties it to a Romantic
notion of the virtues of pre-industrial society. Carrell focuses on the An-
glican High Church and Christian Socialist movements in Britain as being
a major force behind many American settlements' work. The organization
of Episcopal laywomen into the Society of the Companions of the Holy
Cross was a move which, in Carrell's opinion, had an enormous effect on
maintaining a religious focus in the face of increased secularization. She
lists, as members of the Society, Vida Scudder and Helen Dudley of Den-
ison House in Boston, Ellen Starr of Hull House in Chicago, and Mary
Simkhovitch of Greenwich House in New York, all of whom considered
themselves to be Christian Socialists.

According to Carrell, this High Church movement fostered the resident
workers' Romantic notion of the evils and dangers of industrialism, which

they had gleaned from the writings of Morris, Ruskin, Arnold, Browning, Carlyle, and Tolstoy. John Rousmaniere agrees that the Romantics were influential among American settlement resident workers, in consequence of which the latter sought to fill the need of their industrially-victimized neighbors by promoting virtue and work, and by providing entertainment and a proper home life. As a result, notes Daniel Levine, resident workers such as Jane Addams were motivated by the ideal of human unity and the need to foster the integrity of the individual, or what James Dougherty characterizes as the desire for the cultivation of the whole person.

It may be useful to interrupt the essay at this point in order to make a few observations and explain how the author acquired this information about the various historians she is discussing. Note how she proceeds from the traditional interpretation of the settlement movement (that offered by Jane Addams and others) to the revisionist views of later scholars. She groups together in one or two paragraphs historians who take the same *general* approach but also points out differences among them in regard to emphasis and interpretation. Thus so far the reader has been led from a consideration of the religious motive to the question of the backgrounds of settlement workers to the role of Romanticism in their thinking, all organized within a discussion of the various historians of the subject.

In order to extract this kind of information, one must read the book, article, or essay with that purpose in mind. Titles, as we have seen, usually give some idea of what the author is discussing. Tables of contents, prefaces, introductions, and conclusions provide other ways to get a quick idea of an author's orientation. If this is done before reading the work (and it is *not* always necessary to read a work in its entirety), you will be much better able to look for and find especially significant passages that reveal the author's approach or methodology. As you do this, take notes on 5 × 8 or 4 × 6 notecards, including precise page references to passages you may wish to cite or quote. The same care must be given to taking full and precise notecards of your reading as that given to your bibliography card file (see the section on Notetaking in the next chapter). Let us now return to the historiographic essay.

> While taking into account the religious and Romantic factors which influenced women in the late nineteenth century, certain other historians have focused on the importance of college education, naming it as the dominant factor in women's decisions to take up residence in settlement

houses. It is estimated that nearly ninety percent of all resident workers
had attended college, more than eighty percent had a bachelor's degree
or the equivalent, and over fifty percent had done graduate work. The
median age of a resident worker was twenty-five, most were unmarried,
and the greatest number of resident workers were college-educated women
from middle-class homes.

John Rousmaniere takes issue with historians who consider only the
religious influences and implications of settlement work. He views the
American settlement as a novel structure set up and run successfully by
college-educated women who operated in actual or near peer groups. He
gives as evidence for his argument the fact that Vassar, Smith, and Wellesley colleges provided all of the sixteen first-year resident workers in American settlements, almost half of the 1889–1894 resident workers, and a
majority of the long-term resident workers.

Rousmaniere places the greatest emphasis on the well-rounded education offered at Vassar, Smith, and Wellesley which encouraged young
women to balance their studies with extracurricular activities, to form
small, independent peer groups, to be exposed to what was for that period
advanced social thought stressing women's activities outside the home,
and to realize "their uniqueness and superiority to other women." Such
college-educated women, he argues, were motivated to enter settlement
work in order to express their feelings of uniqueness and mission. For
that reason, according to Rousmaniere, Vida Scudder founded the College
Settlement Association in 1890 as a voluntary association of college women
rather than merely an association of settlement workers.

Elizabeth Carrell agrees with Rousmaniere on this last point and elab-
orates upon it in a discussion of Vida Scudder's address to the Association
of Collegiate Alumnae in which Scudder's theme was the uniqueness and
duty of the "true woman" who was also an intellectual. What Scudder
focused on, Carrell claims, was the opportunity for college women to
develop their sense of sisterhood through residency.

A consideration of the preceding paragraphs is in order. The author
has introduced the topic of education and shows how some of the
historians of the settlement movement have looked at resident workers
in terms of their educational backgrounds. She takes this opportunity
to bring forth some of the evidence used, citing, for example, John
Rousmaniere's statistics regarding the college backgrounds of the women
resident workers and Elizabeth Carrell's use of Vida Scudder's address
to the Association of Collegiate Alumnae. Historiographic essays always
benefit from explaining the kind of evidence used by the historians. As

you read and take notes be on the lookout for the evidence used and the manner in which it is deployed.

That college women were able to find a niche in Victorian society while struggling within the established stereotypes is the crucial issue for Jill Conway. Her treatment of the motivation of women resident workers is not greatly unlike Rousmaniere's, yet Conway dismisses as less significant any real Romantic impulse for the migration of middle-class women to the inner cities. In what might be described as a radical feminist interpretation, Conway states bluntly that settlement work functioned as "a social cure for the neurotic ills of privileged young women in America because their ailments were socially induced." What resulted was that meeting the needs of the urban poor was secondary to the settlements' function of fulfilling the psychological needs of young, unmarried resident workers whose society taught them to seek roles as maternal figures.

In another attempt to analyze the psychological motivations of women resident workers, two distinct theories on parental influence seem to have emerged. One theory suggests that the majority of women reformers in general were overwhelmingly shaped by their fathers' standards, noting Jane Addams, Florence Kelley, Julia Lathrop, and Emily Balch as examples. [The reference here is to Elizabeth Carrell's dissertation.]

However, that theory is rejected by Ellen Lagemann and Blanche Wiessen Cook who, as historians of the women's movement, prefer to interpret influence in terms of woman-to-woman relationships. Lagemann argues that the majority of women reformers and resident workers believed from childhood that the family should be the emotional and social center of one's life, that the home should be both a sanctuary and a school, and that a parent, especially a mother, should be a teacher, guardian, and friend. A senior resident worker (in almost all cases a woman) served as a mentor to a junior resident worker in much the same way, according to Lagemann, as a mother related to her daughter. In fact, she says, the mentor relationship was the logical extension of the intimacy between mother and daughter that the Victorian woman experienced during childhood.

Cook expresses a more radical feminist perspective on woman-to-woman relationships. She accuses male historians of interpreting Freud through a Victorian prism and of painting a picture of resident workers as asexual or as afraid of losing their femininity. She is confident that women resident workers enjoyed the support, love, and loyalty of other women as well as the support of men. Cook characterizes those women as more secure in themselves and their work, and attributes that confidence to the development of female support networks which linked the resident workers of many different settlements, allowing them to develop their administra-

tive ability and capacity for independence. As examples of the success of
those networks she cites the lifelong relationships between Lillian Wald
and Lavinia L. Dock, and between Jane Addams and Mary Rozet Smith.

In these paragraphs, the author has described a variety of interpretations offered by historians regarding the motives of women residents.
Some of these interpretations depend upon an assessment of the Victorian family and the way in which its structure and values operated
to socialize young women. Father-daughter and mother-daughter relationships are adduced as critical by some historians in the formation
of values and the choice of careers by women. It will be noted that
some of these explanations might be described as psychohistorical in
nature. This is the final selection from the essay, this one dealing with
the impact of the settlement houses on those they served.

As regards the education provided new immigrants, Allen Davis and
Daniel Levine both remark on the importance of vocational training and
the development of social skills as attempts to teach individuals the importance of their work toward a finished product, and the place of that
product in the total economy. Christopher Lasch is critical of such an
educational scheme and argues that it was too conservative, anti-intellec-
tual, and served only as a means of social control which was eventually
reduced to teaching the skills of good citizenship.

Of the historians who claim that settlement workers and charities had
practically the same motives, Paul McBride considers settlement work to
have been no more than an attempt to make immigrants over into middle-
class Americans. He argues that resident workers sought to achieve a
cultural monism which demanded conformity at the expense of the immigrants' native cultures. McBride's criticism is most clearly directed toward
what he considers to have been the condescending, paternalistic, and
elitist attitudes of the resident workers, whom he characterizes as the
disseminators of propaganda for a subtle brand of social imperialism.
Lillian Wald, in McBrides's opinion, was one of only a few resident workers who sought in any way to preserve the immigrants' historical interests
in their own cultures. All others, he goes on, operated with the purpose
of substituting middle-class American economic and social values for Old
World traditions. Likewise, certain groups of immigrants, namely southern
Europeans, were considered by resident workers to be dangerous threats
to the American way of life.

Other historians have commented that settlement workers organized
social clubs, introduced arts and crafts, and taught classes in homemaking
which were designed to aid new immigrants in adapting to American

culture. But, they point out, the fact remains that in doing so the resident workers' notions of American cultural superiority and of moral evolution implied a contradiction of their notions of human unity and the destruction of social and class barriers. [The reference here is to the Davis and Levine books.]

In quoting most of the body of this essay, passages dealing with historians' differing views of the comparisons of American and British settlements and the attitude of settlement workers to World War I have been omitted. This was done in the interest of space and because the paragraphs that have been quoted amply illustrate the structure and function of a historiographic essay. Partly for the same reason the concluding paragraphs have been omitted. An effective conclusion is of course a crucial ingredient of all papers; a good conclusion for a historiographic essay sums up clearly the various themes and approaches in the writing about the topic. The reader should be reminded, in brief compass, of the various subtopics into which the subject has been divided and the differing interpretations that have emerged. After this summary review of the literature, the author may wish to pinpoint certain facets of the topic that have been neglected or given short shrift.

## Alternative Approaches

In considering this study of the writings about the American settlement movement, it should not be imagined that the structure and style of all historiographic essays conforms to this one. There are other successful methods of writing this kind of essay. The nature of the topic will to some extent entail differences in approach. A military, political, or diplomatic subject might benefit from a substantially different structure. More important, even the topic of the American settlement movement can be well-treated historiographically with quite different methods.

It will be noted that the author chose to organize the material topically—that is, looking in turn at religion, education, women, immigrants, and so on. This proved quite effective. Within each subtopic she was able to discuss and compare the views of several historians. And because many topics shaded over into others (e.g., religion into education), an effective transition device was afforded her. However, it would also have been possible to structure the paper chronologically.

Beginning with the rather self-congratulatory literature written by participants in the movement (Addams et al.), she could have moved to the critical, in some cases "debunking" history written in the 1960s and early 1970s by authors such as Lasch and Levine. One advantage of employing a chronological perspective would have been to highlight how the treatment of the topic has fallen more and more into the orbit of women's history since the 1970s, with a wealth of new perspectives provided from that general vantage point. There is no rigid formula. Whether the approach is topical, chronological, or some combination depends on many factors, not the least of which is simply the author's preference.

A number of valuable insights should emerge from the writing of a historiographic essay. For one thing, it is an especially valuable device for developing and honing library research skills. Even more important, it encourages, indeed compels, the reading of history with an eye to understanding the approaches and methods of various historians. It enables one to think historiographically, an essential attainment for those who are serious about understanding history as an intellectual discipline. It is also an invaluable frame of mind for undertaking a major research paper, which will be examined in the next chapter.

# 5

# Engaging with Primary Sources: The Research Paper

IN THE last chapter, some effective methods of researching and writing the historiographic essay were examined; in this chapter the same process for the research paper will be considered. The former is concerned almost entirely with secondary sources, while in the latter all available primary sources, as well as the relevant secondary works, are used. Moreover, a research paper is usually lengthier than a historiographic essay. A typical form in which the undergraduate encounters it is in the senior thesis—an extensive project sometimes extending over an entire academic year, often taught on a seminar basis. A term paper in an upper-division course may sometimes be extensive enough to qualify as a research paper, although usually it is shorter and based on relatively few sources. Still, many of the skills and methods requisite for the longer project will be applicable to the term paper as well.

A senior thesis or similar extensive research project can be considered a "capstone" experience of an undergraduate major in history. It brings together the knowledge and insights gained from previous courses, recently acquired research skills, and one's growing powers of analysis, imagination, and expression. It offers the opportunity to move beyond a somewhat passive mode of learning into the critical and analytical mode of the self-directed research scholar. Approached with the proper attitude of adventure and determination, it can prove to be the most valuable and memorable academic experience of one's undergraduate career.

## Searching for a Viable Topic

It is important to have a topic of manageable scope and, as with the historiographic essay, this will almost certainly entail some pruning of the subject originally selected. But there are also considerations that are peculiar to the research paper. For example, it is usually necessary to choose a topic for which primary sources are accessible. By checking on the availability of published sources (or even close-at-hand manuscripts that one is allowed to use) early in the research process, a potentially large waste of time can be averted. Otherwise, diligent research in the library catalog and various indexes might yield an admirable array of secondary works but few if any primary sources. It is possible, of course, that the nature of the topic or the instructor's guidelines might render this paucity of primary sources acceptable, but one must be sure to check.

At this point it might be objected that I have drawn too firm a distinction between primary and secondary sources. Is it not the case that the authors of books, articles, and essays often quote freely from primary materials? And in writing a research paper, is it not perfectly acceptable to use and even quote the sources used by other historians? After all, the amount of primary source material that could be culled in this fashion from a couple of dozen secondary works might be considerable. The answer is that while it *is* acceptable to quote material quoted by others, this should be done sparingly and is not a substitute for reading through and selecting from a much larger mass of primary materials.

The rule is always to use the fullest, best-edited collection of any primary source available. Under this rule, the most "nutritious" source would be the raw, unedited manuscripts or published editions of these sources in which the manuscripts are reproduced in their entirety. From that state there is a descending scale in which more and more highly processed sources are used (as in *The Selected Letters of* . . . .). If the analogy to food sources is to be pursued, by the time one reaches source material quoted in secondary works, it should be considered not just as highly processed but as having already been consumed and digested. In dealing with primary sources, the historian's task is to select representative and illustrative documents from as large a collection as possible. Becoming a sensitive, skillful, and efficient analyst of source material is a vital part of training to be a historian.

## Finding Primary Sources

Since the process of finding secondary works was explored in the last two chapters, we can concentrate here on the process of locating primary sources. One method that was mentioned earlier, for finding collections of documents in book form, was to look in the subject heading cards for the topic in the library catalog to see if there were subject heading cards with the word "Sources" added. If the topic is biographical, or has significant biographical components, looking under the person's name in both the author and subject catalog is a good idea.

Another effective method is to look for published bibliographies on the topic, which may be in the form of essays or articles as well as books. Some of the major places to find the titles of published bibliographies are the subject heading catalog, the *Guide to Reference Books* edited by Sheehy (*see* Chapter 3), and the *Bibliographic Index*. Many published bibliographies have a section on primary sources. Most will have a much larger chronological or topical sweep than your topic and you will need to look up your time period or topic in the table of contents or index. A prime example is *The Harvard Guide to American History,* an excellent reference source for both primary and secondary sources. If you are working on some aspect of the American Revolution, for example, looking under that section in the *Harvard Guide* will refer you to several useful collections of published documents. You may also wish to investigate the availability of local manuscript sources and whether or not your library has an oral history collection.

In searching for published collections of primary sources, one should consult the bibliographies and footnotes of the secondary sources, as well as doing some creative shelf browsing. In many historical monographs, the bibliographies at the end of the book are divided into primary and secondary sources. The former is sometimes further subdivided into manuscript and published sources. In articles and essays, be sure to mine the footnotes for references to published sources. As for shelf browsing, it can be quite effective with regard to primary sources, especially if you are in the stage of still searching for a topic. If, for example, you decided to do a research paper on modern India but had not refined the topic beyond that, scanning the library stacks on the history of India might reveal the massive, multivolume *Collected Works of Mahatma Gandhi.* The availability of this source could serve to point you toward a manageable topic, one that would probably but not necessarily be biographical in nature.

Finally, if the period you are studying falls during the last century or so, you may want to research newspapers or periodicals contemporary with the events being studied. *The Times* (London) and *The*

*New York Times* are widely available on microfilm, and the library's Reference Room should have the indexes that will allow you to access these papers for material on particular topics or persons. Many other newspapers are also available, both on microfilm and as bound copies, but the indexes to them that do exist usually do not go back very far in time. In regard to magazine articles from the period under investigation, *Poole's Index* and the *Reader's Guide to Periodical Literature* will open up the riches of nineteenth- and twentieth-century periodical publications of a more popular bent.

## Approaching the Reading

As you accumulate useful titles for your topic, be sure to fill out 3 × 5 bibliography cards, using different colors for primary and secondary sources. It is unnecessary, indeed inadvisable, to defer reading until one has accumulated the entire list of sources. As was noted in the last chapter, it is a good idea to begin reading something immediately so as to gain some command over the basic factual detail and to assist in refining the scope of the topic. It is best to begin reading the secondary works, because without some factual grasp of the topic, it will not be possible to analyze the primary sources effectively. Also, it is necessary to be aware of some of the historiographic dimensions of the subject first. This entails following the kind of procedure discussed in the last chapter for a historiographic essay. When you have gained an understanding of the kinds of questions posed and approaches taken by other historians, you will be much more skilful with the primary sources.

It should not be thought that I am advising a "hands off" policy on primary materials until all the secondary works have been digested. To begin with, such stern counsel would be hypocritical, since I never observe it myself. On the contrary, whenever I undertake a new project I can hardly wait to get my hands on the primary sources. Moreover, it would not be a good idea. In a research paper you will be involved in understanding the secondary works historiographically as well as analyzing the primary sources. These two processes, if not quite simultaneous, are at least interwoven. When questions are fresh in your mind from reading another historian's account, that is a good time to plunge into the primary sources. Sudden, unexpected insights and connections can occur by varying your reading in this fashion.

Another advantage of making an early foray into the primary materials is that many of them are direct, vivid, and dramatic. Alternating them with books, articles, and essays by other historians is a refreshing change of pace and an excellent device for maintaining a high level of interest in the subject. The same thing should apply to your reading of secondary works. It is not necessary to plod through one weighty tome cover to cover before starting another. There is no reason why you should not be working on several books at the same time. The main thing is not to adopt an overly rigid methodology. It is important to keep a fresh, lively attitude and to enjoy the process. Experiment with different ways of doing your reading until you find one that works best for you.

## Notetaking

As you read, always have a stack of 5 × 8 or 4 × 6 notecards at hand. The 3 × 5 cards used for bibliographies are too small for effective notetaking. Many students and not a few scholars prefer to use spiral notebooks, but these have a number of drawbacks. Notes kept in this fashion on consecutive pages might work well enough for the relatively few sources consulted in a typical term paper, but they tend to prove restrictive and inefficient for larger projects, in all but the most expert hands. The major drawback is the lack of flexibility. With a notebook, one will not be able to aggregate notes relating to the same subtopic. When the time arrives to write that portion of the paper a very frustrating search through the notebook would be required.

Notecards, on the other hand, can be segregated into stacks based on the facet of the subject to which they refer. Even if you divided a notebook into sections for each subtopic, it would still be inflexible, for it frequently happens that after the research for a project is completed, you decide to divide the subject into a quite different set of subtopics than originally planned. If all the notes were taken in a notebook, you would be confronted with the problem of switching back and forth to find notes on each of the new subtopics. With cards, it is supremely easy—you simply reshuffle them to correspond to the new subtopics. You can arrange the sequence of cards relating to each subtopic to reflect the sequence of points you will write about. Another advantage is that merely glancing at the size of each group of cards can indicate whether you need more material on a certain topic or should aggregate it with another, further subdivide it, or perhaps delete it altogether.

Cards should be kept in some kind of file box, preferably with tabbed file separators identifying the cards for each subtopic. It is also a good idea to place some kind of identifying word or mark on the top line of each card, so that if they should ever be dropped or scattered, they can be quickly resegregated. Beyond this minimal identifying mark (which might be simply a letter or number) there should be a brief description on the first line, allowing the contents to be identified at a glance without having to read it all. This will save a good deal of time when you start writing or decide to segregate the cards differently from your original scheme.

Having considered the mechanics of notetaking, the substance of the process needs to be examined. Students are often baffled as to how many and what types of notes they should take. Should one record each and every "fact" one reads? If so, the stack of notecards would swell to unmanageable proportions before the first book was read. There is a large amount of factual detail about the topic you will encounter in your reading that does not warrant the time and effort for a note. In the course of reading a large number of historians' accounts as well as primary sources you will acquire a familiarity with the major events, processes, and persons that constitute the subject. One should take notes only on those facts that there is reason to think will be necessary in the later analysis of the subject and the writing of the paper. On the other hand, being too sparing in one's notetaking will leave a paucity of material when that time arrives. Obviously it is a question of acquiring a sense of balance, something that comes with practice.

Putting certain facts on cards for later retrieval and analysis is only one of the purposes of notetaking. Another is to record the views of other historians regarding the topic. These might be described as historiographic notes. Remember that in the research paper you will not only illuminate the topic by the use of primary sources, but should also explain to readers at least to some extent the historiographic dimensions of the topic. Another purpose is to record those primary sources, or some portion of them, that you may want to quote or cite in the paper.

Finally, you should take notes on your own thoughts and reflections while reading. This is part of the creative process in research. Perhaps some comparison suddenly occurs to you, or a particular way that you would like to analyze certain documents, when you get around to writing the paper. Do not count on remembering these insights later. Write them down, either on separate cards or as bracketed inserts on the cards containing notes on the material in question. It is also an excellent idea to keep a separate small notebook for the purpose of recording your more general, overarching ruminations as well as to make notes about things to be checked, verified, or further explored.

It is perhaps best at this point to illustrate the process of notetaking by quoting a note of my own. The project in question was research for an article on John Richard Green, who, you may recall from the first chapter, was the author of the very influential *Short History of the English People* (1874). In that part of my research dealing with the impact of the *Short History,* I came across an article written just after Green's death by a scholar who had worked with Green during the latter's tenure as a Church of England clergyman. I was struck by one passage in particular and took the following note:

---

*Popularity of Short History–1883*

"When men leaving Oxford wished to improve their minds, if they were rich they traveled, and if they were poor they read Green's Short History."

—Philip Lyttleton Gell,
"John Richard Green,"
Contemporary Review 39 (1883): 738.

---

Several points should be observed about this notecard. It is a quotation from a primary source since it was written by a contemporary and friend of Green. I selected it partly because it had a nice ring to it and was "atmospheric"—that is, it conveyed the tone and style of the Victorian intellectual circles in which Green moved. The heading tells me at a glance what the card is about and allows it to be filed with other cards on the same subtopic. I also took care to cite the source and page number for this quotation (my actual card has only the simple notation "Gell, p. 738" since I already had a bibliography card for this article with a complete citation).

It is also quite a short note, and it might be thought that the vacant space on the card could be used for other notes. This, however, would violate a cardinal principle of notetaking—only one fact, thought, idea, or quotation per card. To do otherwise is to undermine the flexibility of the card system. The final thing that should be said about this card is that I did not end up using it. When I got around to writing the article,[1] I decided, somewhat reluctantly, to omit it. The focus of the piece had changed from my original intent, and the quote seemed peripheral and unnecessary. You will almost certainly take a good many more notes than you actually use in writing the paper, but this is inherent in the scholarly process. A thoughtful, judicious selection of material from your reading will be followed by a thoughtful, judicious selection from your notecards when it comes time to write.

## The Outline and Structure of the Paper

Well before you are finished with research and are ready to write, you should begin developing an outline of the paper. It is important to give this matter some thought even at the start of your research. Although any outline you come up with at this point will necessarily be tentative and undeveloped, it will nonetheless launch you into the process of thinking structurally and will help you to direct your research efficiently. As with all papers, the major divisions are the introduction, the body of the paper, and the conclusion. It is with the outline of the body of the paper that you should chiefly concern yourself. Initially you will simply be blocking in a few major topics, but as you continue to read, think, and take notes, the outline will develop accordingly. The outline should in fact continue to be amended even during the writing phase. One of the most counterproductive postures you can adopt is to imagine that your outline is at some stage chiseled on stone tablets. You must

---

[1]Anthony Brundage, "John Richard Green and the Church: The Making of a Social Historian," *The Historian* 35 (1972): 32–42.

be free at any time throughout the process to make changes, sometimes of major proportions.

The fully developed outline is the blueprint for the sequence of paragraphs that will constitute your paper. Just as the various topics and subtopics in the outline are related to paragraphs and clusters of paragraphs in the paper, they are also related to the notecards that you are filling out, arranging, and classifying. Your notecards, in fact, are an important key to developing an effective outline. When each note-card is filled out, there is a brief entry on the top line describing the contents. When cards dealing with the same thing are aggregated, they provide one of the topics or subtopics. The number of cards in each group will indicate how much material there is on each subtopic and will suggest if further subdivision is needed. It may be that there are only a few cards on the particular subtopic, which requires a decision about whether to do additional research in that area, to merge that subtopic with something else, or perhaps to drop it altogether. Each time this happens, the outline should be amended accordingly.

A recognition of the interrelationship between clusters of notecards and the items on the outline will help keep some sense of balance and symmetry to the project. But an outline does not simply reflect the noted material that has been accumulated. It should also be a sequence of topics and subtopics, each one of which leads smoothly into the next. That is, the outline establishes a structure for the natural and graceful set of linkages that the completed paper should exhibit. A careful look at the evolving outline can alert you to harsh disjunctions and allow you to rearrange sequences to permit an easy transition from one topic to another.

## Some Elements of Effective Writing

"Always start at the beginning" may not be the best advice to offer someone engaged in a research paper. In many cases, the introduction is best left in a relatively incomplete state until the body of the paper and possibly even the conclusion are completed. As has been seen, it is very likely that the focus of the topic will shift somewhat, not only during the research phase but even during the writing. Nonetheless, a couple of functions of a good introduction should be noted. First, it should clearly inform the reader about the nature and scope of the

paper. This might include something on the historiography of the subject, along with an indication of the approach being taken. Another
important function of a good introduction is to engage the reader's
interest. Clarity is always an excellent means to this end. Some writers
start with a vivid passage describing a central event or process in order
to create atmosphere and draw the reader into the topic, then go on
to describe the scope of the paper. This is not appropriate in all cases,
but for many topics it can provide an effective beginning.

An impressive use of this device can be seen in the opening paragraphs
of *The Crucial Decade,* Eric F. Goldman's classic study of the United
States following World War II. Consider how powerfully the author
creates the atmosphere of 1945 in a few deft narrative paragraphs:

> A U.S. Radio monitor in a little frame house in Oregon caught the first
> hint. The Japanese were interested in peace, the Domei broadcast said,
> provided that the prerogatives of the Emperor would not be "prejudiced."
> Then came two days of diplomacy, a few hours of false armistice, more
> waiting through an interminable weekend. Finally, on Tuesday, August
> 14, 1945, reporters were summoned to the Oval Room of the White
> House. President Truman glanced at the clock to make sure he was holding
> to the agreement of simultaneous announcement in Washington, London,
> and Moscow. At exactly 7 P.M. he began reading: Late that afternoon a
> message had been received from the Japanese Government which "I deem
> . . . full acceptance of . . . unconditional surrender."
>
> Across America the traditional signs of victory flared and shrieked. In
> Los Angeles, yelling paraders commandeered trolley cars, played leapfrog
> in the middle of Hollywood Boulevard, hung Hirohito from scores of
> lampposts. Salt Lake City thousands snakedanced in a pouring rain and a
> St. Louis crowd, suddenly hushing its whistles and tossing aside the con-
> fetti, persuaded a minister to hold services at 2 A.M. New York City,
> hardly unaccustomed to furor, amazed itself. With the first flash of V-J,
> up went the windows and down came the torn telephone books, the hats,
> bottles, bolts of silk, books, wastebaskets, and shoes, more than five thou-
> sand tons of jubilant litter. Whole families made their way to Times Square
> until two million people were milling about, breaking into snatches of the
> conga, hugging and kissing anybody in sight, greeting each twinkle of V-J
> news on the *Times* electric sign with a cheer that roared from the East
> River to the Hudson. The hoopla swirled on into the dawn, died down,
> broke out again the next afternoon, finally subsided only with another
> midnight.
>
> Americans had quite a celebration and yet, in a way, the celebration
> never really rang true. People were so gay, so determinedly gay. The nation

was a carnival but the festivities, as a reporter wrote from Chicago, "didn't seem like so much. It was such a peculiar peace. . . . And everybody talked of 'the end of the war,' not of 'victory.' " The President himself spoke with a mixed tone. When the crowds around the White House chanted: "We want Harry," he appeared beaming with Bess on his arm and proclaimed this "a great day." His face quickly sobered as he added warnings of an "emergency" ahead—a crisis "as great . . . as December 7, 1941." At V-J, 1945, the United States was entering the newest of its eras in a curious, unprecedented jumble of moods.[2]

Goldman not only gives us vivid narrative here, but also delineates the atmosphere of 1945 and hints at its complexity. Criticisms of this type of approach as being too "popular" or "journalistic" are sometimes heard. In response, it might be said that among the various possible reactions to reading Goldman's introductory paragraphs, closing the book seems the least likely.

Acquiring and maintaining a reader's interest should be a high priority for all historians, not just in the introduction but throughout the work. It is true, of course, that many topics do not readily lend themselves to the kind of anecdotal treatment just described. It is also true that telling a story well is only a part of the historian's calling, and not necessarily the highest part. Imposing pattern and meaning on a jumble of events is the historian's central task. This often requires a tone of dispassionate analysis and the use of generalization and abstraction rather than the relating of an exciting narrative. Obviously, these portions of one's work can either be well written or poorly written. While readers should not expect to be kept "entertained" all the time, they do have the right to as much incisiveness, clarity, and wit as you can muster.

Attention to mechanics (such as an effective outline) has an obviously beneficial effect on your written work. A clear, straightforward structure in which each section is designed to lead naturally into the next is essential. Things are not quite so clear when it comes to effective style. Here we are dealing with such matters as syntax and word choice, in which many different "correct" choices are possible. Furthermore, writing style is, or should be, as distinctive as personality. One way your writing is sure to undergo improvement is through the active and critical reading of many well-written histories. By taking care to note how

[2]Eric F. Goldman, *The Crucial Decade and After. America, 1945–1960* (New York: Vintage Books, © 1961), 3–4. Reprinted by permission of Alfred A. Knopf, Inc.

authors structure their works and deploy language effectively, you can apply these insights to your own writing.

There are, of course, some frequently cited injunctions such as avoiding long, convoluted sentences or short, choppy ones. But such admonitions are qualified. What is meant is that a *succession* of such sentences should be avoided. The judicious use of the complex or very brief sentence enlivens one's writing and is a relief to the eye and ear. Such stylistic "rules" can only be general guidelines, which the confident writer will not hesitate to violate when the occasion demands. There are some sound practices that enhance word choice, such as a ready resort to the dictionary and thesaurus. One of the major ways to improve writing style is being willing to undertake multiple revisions of your work. Whatever your expressive abilities and the facility with which you write, there is no substitute for careful editing and reworking—a process that will be considered in more detail later in the chapter.

## An Open Mind and Intellectual Honesty

In addition to effective structure and style, concerns shared equally by writers in all subjects, historians should be especially concerned with intellectual honesty. They need to be genuinely impartial in selecting, analyzing, and presenting evidence. Most of us like to think of ourselves as impartial and fair-minded, but deploying this attitude to good effect in research and writing is not as simple as it sounds. Even if a topic is new to us, we usually start with some slight knowledge of it and some interpretation of it, however hazy and unformed. This, indeed, is a good starting point. At an early stage of your research, ask: What do I know about this subject and what do I consider its significance? Jot down your answer, return to it periodically, and use it as a method of guarding against the *unconscious* tendency of looking for and seeing only that evidence that bolsters your preconceptions.

Just as we must guard against partiality in selecting evidence, the same care must be taken in analyzing it. Primary sources need to be treated with respect as well as skepticism. If you proceed like a trial lawyer or a debater, as though you are involved in an adversarial format, you will end up amassing only that evidence favorable to your side and torturing its meaning to fit a predetermined outcome. Remaining open-minded is crucial to being an effective researcher; it also helps insure that one's ideas and one's work will develop in exciting and unanticipated ways. This is not to say that historians should avoid assertiveness in their interpretation of events or refrain from debates with other scholars. As has been seen, it is precisely these characteristics that make history the lively, dynamic, and valuable discipline it is. What is important is that our firmly held convictions be the *result* of our scholarly labors and not a set of prejudices resolutely fortified by turning a blind eye to contrary evidence.

## Quoting and Footnoting

One commonly observed feature of student research papers is the tendency to overquote. There are no doubt many reasons for this rather fulsome brandishing of the words of others. The least charitable explanation is that it seems an expeditious way of filling the requisite number of pages for the paper, but this does not account for more than a handful of cases. More common is the notion that generous chunks of primary source material will, in addition to functioning as evidence, impart atmosphere to the paper. This is sometimes the case, but only if the material is evocative, well-stated, and appropriate. Even then, the rule should be to quote only as much of a passage as is necessary without destroying or distorting the meaning of the longer document from which it is excerpted. Otherwise, one should simply describe or paraphrase the contents of the document. Overly lengthy or ill-chosen quotations impede the text and weary the reader. Quotations should not be allowed to become roadblocks in the smooth flow of historical narrative and analysis.

With these caveats in mind, let us consider some of the mechanics of quotation. When you have found a passage that might be used in the paper, fill out a notecard, indicating the precise reference to the source. If you are uncertain just how much of the quote will be used, play it safe and note an extended passage. You can make the choice later about how much of it to insert in the paper. Often, you will find that there are various portions of a document you want to use, separated by material that is extraneous to your purpose. In this case, you can omit the unwanted material provided that you: (a) do not distort the meaning of the passage or the context in which it appears; and (b) indicate that material has been omitted by the use of ellipsis points.

Examples of the use of ellipsis points are to be seen in the introductory paragraphs of Eric Goldman's *The Crucial Decade,* quoted
above. When Goldman tells of President Truman's announcement of
the Japanese surrender, he quotes only one sentence and prunes it
considerably so that it flows into his narrative: "Late that afternoon a
message had been received from the Japanese Government which 'I
deem ... full acceptance of ... unconditional surrender.' " A couple
of paragraphs later, Goldman again uses ellipsis points to good effect
in quoting the words of a Chicago reporter: "It was such a peculiar
peace.... And everybody talked of 'the end of the war,' not of 'victory.' "

In the first passage the omitted material, indicated by the two sets
of ellipsis points (each consisting of three periods), is within a single
sentence. In the second passage the reader knows the omitted material
is more than one sentence because there is a period immediately after
the word "peace" and before the ellipsis points. Note also that the
word "And" is capitalized, indicating that in the original source it is
the beginning of another sentence. Did Goldman meet the other re-
quirement of the use of ellipsis points, namely that the omission of
material not distort the meaning of the document? Only a check of the
full sources he used could answer that question. But it is easy to see
how very distorted the meaning *would* have been had the author left
out the final phrase of the Chicago reporter's second sentence, so that
it read: "And everybody talked of 'the end of the war'.... " This is
an accurate quote, and ellipsis points are used, but eliminating the
phrase "not of 'victory' " utterly confounds and obscures the original
meaning.

Ellipsis points allow one to quote only those portions of a document
that are of use. They permit a very flexible tailoring of quoted material
so that it meshes with your writing without impeding the narrative flow.
This smooth integration of primary material with one's work is easiest
when the material quoted is brief—a sentence or less. There are times,
of course, when you need to quote lengthier passages, perhaps as much
as a paragraph or so. This is bound to impede the flow of the narrative
at least slightly, but if you are satisfied that it will enhance the paper,
you should have no compunctions about going ahead. If the quotation
is only a couple of lines, simply set it off with a colon and quotation
marks. For passages that are going to be over three or four lines, you
should use a block quotation, in which the passage is single-spaced and

indented from the left margin. With a block quote, quotation marks are *not* used, since it is clear from the additional indentation and single-spacing that material is being quoted. For a quotation of a page or more (to be used very sparingly), it is often advisable to insert it as an appendix to the paper.

The discussion of footnoting can be divided into what needs to be footnoted and how it should be done. In regard to the former, most students are fully aware that all quotations must be footnoted; it is the footnoting of other material that raises problems. Should each "fact" be footnoted? To do so would be to encumber one's text with thick clusters of numbers and a corresponding long list of notes at the bottom of each page (or at the end of the paper, if endnotes are being used). The purpose of footnoting is to allow the reader to check on the accuracy of the quotations, citations, and assertions. One should not footnote a major fact that is well-known and unchallenged, such as "President Lincoln was assassinated by John Wilkes Booth" or "The Normans invaded England in 1066." Nor is it necessary to footnote most of those "smaller" facts about events or details in a person's life that the reader can easily check by consulting some of the works in the paper's bibliography. But when such a fact is being emphasized or used for evidence, and certainly when it is in dispute, one should use a footnote. Also a footnote should be used for citing another work, primary or secondary, even if not directly quoting from it.

There are two basic types of footnotes (or endnotes)—reference foot-notes and content footnotes. The former is the documentation of a quotation, citation, or assertion that simply cites the bibliographic information on the source, including the page number (if applicable). This is the most common type and little needs to be said about it except for the necessity of formatting it correctly. There are several style manuals used in the historical profession, and it is important to find out which one should be used and then stick to it consistently. The University of Chicago *Manual of Style*[3] is the most commonly used, but the student must be sure to check with the instructor. The system of formatting used determines such matters as the manner and sequence in which publication data are stated, how to make subsequent references to the same work, and so on.

---

[3]The most convenient reference work for using the University of Chicago format is Kate L. Turabian. *A Manual for Writers of Term Papers, Theses, and Dissertations.* 5th edition (Chicago: University of Chicago Press, 1987).

The content footnote requires some explanation. One use is to provide further elaboration on some point made in the paper, without encumbering the text with a digression that may be of only marginal interest to some readers. Digressions in a story are sometimes unavoidable and can be highly interesting, but if they are employed too much the reader's patience and attention begin to wane. It is like listening to a long-winded speaker who insists on giving a wealth of background detail about each component of his story. We not only grow weary; such meanderings cause us to lose track of the point and direction of the story. One of the advantages of the written over the spoken word is that such collateral material can be consigned to a content footnote where, perhaps in a few sentences or a paragraph, additional information can be provided to those readers particularly interested in that point. The body of the text is allowed to remain unencumbered.

A similar use of the content footnote is to provide a brief historiographical discussion on some point without cluttering the text. One may, for example, relate some fact that a few scholars dispute, or offer differing interpretations. This may be combined with a reference footnote—that is, a simple citation to a source in the footnote might be immediately followed by something like: "However, this view has recently been challenged by X, who introduces new evidence which casts some doubt on the genuineness of the draft treaty. See . . ." (here the writer would have the complete citation to the revisionist article by X).

## Editing and Revising

In striving for excellence in written work, there is no substitute for painstaking editing and revising. No matter how good you may feel about the quality of the first draft, a later critical scrutiny is certain to reveal inconsistencies, abrupt transitions, unclear passages, infelicitous expressions, and other matters in need of urgent attention. To a lesser degree, the same will apply to a perusal of the second draft. Rewriting is a critically important phase of the scholarly process, not something that might be squeezed in if one has enough time left before the deadline for submitting the paper. Time is always in short supply for the harried student, so it is essential to plan its use wisely. In addition to leaving time for rewriting, you should, if possible, allow for some "percolation time"—a few days away from research, writing, and rewriting, in which your thoughts can percolate and fresh insights can emerge. It is especially valuable to leave some time between the writing of drafts of the paper and the final version.

In going over your first draft, it is sometimes useful to read it aloud. This brings your ear into the process and allows you to detect more readily those passages that need remedial attention. This is also very helpful in proofreading, because in reading our own work silently, we see what we expect to see, and can easily miss omitted, misspelled, or duplicated words. Having a fellow student listen to or read your work can also be useful, as long as you have reason to believe that he or she has the ability, interest, and candor to comment critically. Sometimes a senior thesis is taught on a seminar basis, in which portions of rough drafts are read aloud to one's fellow students, who then offer constructive criticism (in addition to that of the instructor). These encounters almost invariably prove rewarding and interesting and create a strong atmosphere of mutual support. They are, or can be, microcosms of the "communities of scholars" that exist in the wider historical profession.

The number of drafts you write will depend on many factors, including your writing abilities, the time at your disposal, and the views of your instructor. A word processor will prove an immense advantage in this process, a topic we will examine below. When the body of your paper is in good shape, you can then turn your attention to revising the introduction and conclusion. Now that the body of your paper is in its finished form, you know exactly what it is that you need to introduce and conclude. You can then add the "scholarly apparatus" of endnotes (assuming you are not using actual footnotes) and bibliography. Your instructor will almost certainly have established some guidelines for these, including the style manual to be used for notes and bibliographical entries.

## In Praise of the Word Processor

One of the greatest boons to the serious writer in any field is the word processor. Present users will need no convincing on this point. Many of those not using a word processor simply do not have access to one, but fortunately most colleges and universities are making available in-

creasing numbers of them for use by students. There is, however, a
significant core of resistance, based on computer phobia, unwillingness
to take the time required to use one proficiently, or complacency with
long-established writing habits. Many of us now gratefully using a word
processor counted ourselves formerly in one of these categories (in my
own case, all three). The time needed to learn a word processing system
is usually much shorter than the apprehensive neophyte imagines, a
situation that continues to improve as programs become more and more
"user friendly."

Once the extraordinary speed, efficiency, and flexibility of using a
word processor has been experienced, the thought of writing a lengthy
paper with a typewriter or pen will seem most unpalatable. With a word
processor, frequent and wholesale editing is remarkably simple. Single
words, sentences, paragraphs, whole sections, can be instantly deleted,
amended, or rearranged, and a new, clean version displayed immediately
on the screen. In addition, many programs include a spelling checker
and some have a thesaurus. Other programs can spot things like un-
intentional double words and the frequent use of certain uncommon
words. The unlimited ability to move text around greatly facilitates
experimenting with a number of possible arrangements. In contrast,
just a few such changes on a handwritten or typewritten draft produce
a bewildering and dispiriting jumble of strikeovers, scribbles, arrows,
carets, and interlineations.

Only when the text is to your satisfaction do you need to issue the
print command. Or you can print a few drafts of your work, read them
over later, and make notes for subsequent changes when returning to
the screen and keyboard. With the work saved on a disk, it is never
frozen into some unmalleable form such as a typewritten paper, any
revision of which requires a complete retyping. A major impediment
to revising your work has been eliminated by the computer, permitting
you to produce work of higher quality, in less time, and with a lot
more enjoyment. This must be qualified by the observation that the
word processor is only a tool. If one neglects to use its many remarkable
features, particularly its editing functions, it is little more than a typewriter with a screen. Some parts of the scholarly process are more
interesting and creative than others. The word processor gives us the
*potential* for enhancing and expanding the creative aspects of writing
and revising, while eliminating some of the drudgery. To the extent
that it is used, both writers and readers will be grateful.

# 6

## Conclusion: History and Creativity

IN LEGAL instruments known as Articles of Apprenticeship, commonly used in medieval and early modern England, the phrase that was used to refer to the occupation in question was "art, science, craft, or mystery." This phrase conveys the sense that there were important expressive and creative components to even the most mundane lines of manufacture in the preindustrial age. It is an expression that seems peculiarly appropriate to the historian's calling. However much the practice of history seems to involve the systematic application of certain skills, there are wide, important areas of both research and writing that tap the creative spirit. Recall that the Greeks considered history an important enough expressive field to assign one of the nine Muses to it. The modern historical profession still embraces this traditional identification as a branch of literature, even as it functions in close alliance with the social sciences, or indeed is often classified as one of them. Far from being troubled by this dual identity, most historians glory in it. The point is that whether history is viewed chiefly as a social science or as one of the humanities, its creative dimensions are of central importance.

In the sections of this book dealing with research and writing, the emphasis has been on matters that might be considered mechanical in nature—the use of card catalogs, indexes, and various reference sources, as well as some techniques of reading, notetaking, writing, and revising. One reason for this emphasis is the absolute necessity for students to be well grounded in historical methodology. Another is, quite frankly, that it is much easier to examine systematically the elements of good historical craftsmanship than it is to explain its creative dimensions. Methodology can be dealt with prescriptively but creativity cannot. There are no rules or techniques to being creative, and few creative people in any field can offer much in the way of guidance. Hunches, sudden insights, and inspirations are some of the undoubted manifestations of creativity, but one is tempted to ascribe them to the "mystery" part of the medieval apprenticeship phrase quoted above.

Nonetheless, even if creativity cannot ultimately be explained, it is possible to recognize it, to encourage it, and to extend it. The first and most essential thing is to discard the notion that some people are naturally creative while the rest are forever doomed to being plodders. Whatever mental and psychological processes are involved, they are possessed by everyone. It is possible, of course, for people to convince themselves, or allow others to convince them, that they are somehow deficient in intelligence and imagination. Others may be persuaded that it is not prudent to display such qualities. In many societies past and present, creative impulses are viewed with suspicion, out of fear that they pose a threat to the established order and ways of doing things. Certain religious systems and ideologies, insofar as they claim to possess a monopoly of truth, are also inhospitable to the creative spirit. It is a vital function of education generally, and of universities in particular, to counteract these baneful tendencies.

One of the best ways historians can aid in this endeavor is to insist on the open-endedness of their discipline. It has been one of the purposes of this book to set forth a view of history as dynamic and evolving. Our views of the past evolve as we move into the future and thus acquire an ever-changing vantage point. Like travelers toiling up the side of a mountain (or even descending, if pessimists feel that it is a more appropriate metaphor), we find that the configuration of the landscape behind us has changed each time we turn around. Once prominent features recede into obscurity while others loom into view, and new patterns and relationships can be discerned. A shifting panorama is, after all, one of the things that makes a journey interesting and instructive. It is all too possible, alas, to take a journey without looking around, or to do so in such a cursory fashion that nothing of significance is detected. No one sets out to write a dull, plodding account; one of the best ways to avoid doing so is to keep in mind that even the smallest project of historical inquiry is part of a larger intellectual odyssey.

My insistence on linking creativity with a conception of history as open-ended perhaps raises the old troubling question about whether or not there is such a thing as objective truth. If "everything is relative," what can we really know about the past? Is any one person's version of history as "true" as any other's? The answer is that of course there is objective truth in history. It may be elusive but it is usually accessible and must always be rigorously pursued. Truth in history resides in those ascertainable facts that make up the superstructure of any historical account. Whether or not King Harold of England perished at the hands of Norman invaders in the so-called Battle of Hastings in 1066 can be determined by marshalling every fragment of surviving evidence, assessing each source for its authenticity and reliability, and noting inconsistencies and contradictions. The result of this process is an overwhelming conviction that indeed Harold was killed on that fateful October day. His death has become duly registered as one of those countless facts that constitute the annals of the past. Of course, in some sense it must be considered provisional, that is, subject to being changed should contradictory evidence come to light. Nonetheless, it remains a remarkably "sturdy" fact that, like most other verifiable occurrences, will almost certainly not be altered. Thus we can rest assured that these verified past events will not be plucked away or overturned by someone's whim or fancy.

However, this array of facts, contrary to popular misconceptions, does not constitute history. History is the intellectual discipline that, in addition to discovering, verifying, and describing past events, imposes pattern and meaning upon them. Indeed, the imposing of pattern and meaning are the most important parts of the historian's calling. It is here that revisionism flourishes. Here, too, is the widest scope for the creative insights of the historian. If history is conceived as a fixed chronicle, there is little scope for either creativity or revisionism, which march hand in hand. They must continue to do so if history is to respond to the changing needs and aspirations of the ever-advancing present, along with providing thoughtful anticipations of the future.

# Suggestions for Further Reading

The following short list of books represents only a small portion of the many valuable guides and reference works that might be of service to students of history. Each book is apt to prove valuable for different aspects of research and writing.

Barzun, Jacques, and Henry Graff. *The Modern Researcher.* 4th ed. San Diego: Harcourt, Brace, Jovanovich, 1985. A classic in the field, this lengthy, well-written guide by two masters of the historian's craft is particularly useful for its exploration of the intellectual processes involved in researching and writing history.

Benjamin, Jules R. *A Student's Guide to History.* 4th ed. New York: St. Martin's Press, 1987. This book covers many items of interest to undergraduate history majors, including notetaking at lectures and taking exams as well as research and writing. It also contains a very lengthy and most valuable bibliography of all kinds of historical reference works.

Gilderhus, Mark T. *History and Historians: A Historiographical Introduction.* Englewood Cliffs, New Jersey: Prentice-Hall, 1987. This is a concise, lucid introduction to the history of history writing.

Hexter, J. H. *Doing History.* Bloomington: Indiana University Press, 1971. This book is a lively, somewhat offbeat explication of history as a form of knowledge, its inner dynamics, and its relationship to other disciplines. It stresses the distinctiveness of history and its fundamental differences from the social sciences.

McCoy, F. N. *Researching and Writing in History: A Practical Handbook for Students.* Berkeley and Los Angeles: University of California Press, 1974. This is a step-by-step guide to researching and writing a lengthy history paper. While still useful, some of its sections need updating to reflect changes in titles of some reference sources and to incorporate a treatment of computer searching.

Sanderlin, David. *Writing the History Paper: How to Select, Collect, Interpret, Organize, and Write Your Term Paper.* Woodbury, New York: Barron's Educational Series, 1975. The subtitle accurately reflects the scope of this brief book. The book provides especially good guidance for the details and mechanics of writing.

Steffens, Henry J., and Mary Jane Dickerson. *Writer's Guide: History.* Lexington, Mass.: D. C. Heath, 1978. This book covers many aspects of student research and writing from the short essay to the research paper, using examples of student work.

Strunk, William, Jr., and E. B. White. *The Elements of Style.* 3rd ed. New York: Macmillan, 1979. This explores the subject of writing style with wit, verve, and clarity. It is particularly good on commonly misused words and phrases.

Turabian, Kate L. *A Manual for Writers of Term Papers, Theses, and Dissertations.* 5th ed. Chicago: University of Chicago Press, 1987. Based on the University of Chicago *Manual of Style,* this short reference work covers all aspects of citing and formatting, not just for history and the social sciences, but the natural sciences as well.

*Going to the Sources* was copyedited and proofread by Martha Kreger. Production manager was Judith Almendáriz. The book was typeset by Impressions, Inc., and the first run was printed and bound by Lithocolor Press, Inc.

Cover and book design by Roger Eggers.